Mountain Biking

Michigan

The Best Trails
In
Southern
Michigan

PEGG LEGG
PUBLICATIONS

Other Biking Books From Pegg Legg Publications:

Mountain Biking Michigan:
The Best Trails In Northern Michigan

Cycling Michigan:
The Best Routes In Western Michigan

Cycling Michigan:
The Best Routes In Eastern Michigan

Mountain Biking
Michigan
The Best Trails In Southern Michigan

By Dwain Abramowski and Sandra Davison

PEGG LEGG
PUBLICATIONS

Published by Thunder Bay Press
Production and design by Pegg Legg Publications
Maps by Miller Design and Pegg Legg Publications
Printing by Eerdmans Printing Company, Grand Rapids, MI
Inside photography by Sandra Davison and Dwain Abramowski
Author photo by Tom Gennara

ISBN: 1-88-2376-20-X

Printed in the United States of America

99 100   2 3 4 5 6 7 8

PEGG LEGG
PUBLICATIONS

Holt, Michigan

Acknowledgments

I have the honor of dedicating my portions of this book to all Michigan Mountain Biking Association (MMBA) volunteers who have paid their dues, rolled up their sleeves and have contributed to trail development and maintenance in Michigan. Without reservation, I can say that every single public mountain biking trail opportunity in Michigan has been, in some way, affected by the efforts of MMBA members. If you ride on a public trail you are benefiting from their efforts. This book was made possible by them. The health and well-being of trail access in the future will be directly related to their endeavors.

Michigan has truly phenomenal mountain biking opportunities, as is evident in this book by the number of trails open to the public. Michigan mountain bikers enjoy unparalleled access to multi-use trails as compared to the rest of the country. I hope you enjoy riding these trails. But also make a personal commitment to assist with trail maintenance and development so that the rides you enjoy now will be there for all of us forever.

I especially need to thank my wife, Christina, for working so very hard at a "real job" so that I can write and contribute to the needs of mountain bikers in Michigan.

Dwain Abramowski

Many friends and professionals have contributed to my love of mountain biking and hence to my interest in this book. I wish to recognize my biking friends Randy, Robin, and Dennis for their enthusiasm, patience and help, and for their frequent generosity.

Of course, my Mom and Dad have always been important for their understanding of my wildness and need to be outside, thank you. For his great compassion and generosity (and sobering questions) I thank Dr. Michael Austin. I also am indebted to Linda Peckham who understands more than most people and cultivates where others beat the ground.

I also extend appreciation to the million other people who have shared their love of this sport with me.

Sandra Davison

Mountain Biking
Southern Michigan

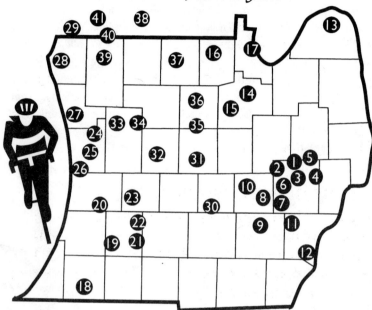

Southeast
1. Holdridge Lakes
2. Seven Lakes
3. Bald Mountain
4. Addison Oaks
5. Ortonville
6. Pontiac Lake
7. Highland
8. Island Lake
9. Pinckney
10. Brighton
11. Maybury
12. Pointe Mouillee

Saginaw Bay
13. Sleeper
14. Shiawasee

15. Ringwood Forest
16. Pine Haven
17. Tobico Marsh

Southwest
18. Lawless
19. Al Sabo
20. Allegan
21. Fort Custer
22. Kellogg Forest
23. Yankee Springs

Lake Michigan
24. Bass River
25. Pigeon Creek
26. Riley Street
27. Hofma
28. Pentwater

29. Whiskey Creek

Heartland
30. Grand River
31. Sleepy Hollow
32. Ionia
33. Cannonsburg Ski
34. Cannonsburg
35. Maple River
36. Jailhouse
37. Deerfield
38. Cool's Farm

NCT
39. Nichlos Lake
40. Bowman Lake
41. Timber Creek

Contents

Introduction

Southeast Michigan

Saginaw Bay

Southwest Michigan

Lake Michigan

Heartland

North Country Trail

Other Trails

Mountain bikers enjoy the trail system at Ionia Recreation Area, between Lansing and Grand Rapids.

Mountain Biking Southern Michigan

When the members of the Holly-Flint Chapter of the Michigan Mountain Biking Association want to go mountain biking...they want to go mountain biking. They want to be out riding, they want to be pumping their way up a steep slope, they want to be following a single track through the autumn woods.

They don't want to be sitting in their cars.

"When I have two hours to spend biking," said one member, "I don't want to waste half of it in a car."

It was that line of thinking that motivated the 70 members of Holly-Flint Chapter of the Michigan Mountain Biking Association (MMBA) to approach officials at the Holly Recreation Area in 1994 about building a trail system close to home. After the local bikers donated more than 700 hours cutting trails, constructing bridges, even mowing the parking area, the Holdridge Lakes Mountain Bicycle Area was unveiled.

The point is, the reason we wrote this guidebook; why spend hours driving up north when some of the best mountain biking in the state is in southern Michigan? As the sport exploded in the early 1990s, so has the number of trail systems and nowhere is that better seen than in southern Michigan where riders, clubs and volunteers were determined to provide mountain biking opportunities close to home.

"In Michigan, we're always so focused on going up north for

recreation," said Jon LaBossiere, manager of the Pinckney Recreation Area, the most popular destination for mountain bikers in southern Michigan. "But I think what we have now in Southeast Michigan is unique in the Midwest. No other area in the state has the variety of (mountain biking) trails we have."

As proof LaBossiere points to the Silver Lake parking area in his park, the trailhead for the Potawatomi Trail. On most days cars with Ohio license plates begin showing up after 3 p.m. On a nice weekend there are plates from Indiana and Illinois as well, making Pinckney State Recreation Area something of a Mecca for mountain bikers.

But mountain biking in southern Michigan is more than just riding the rugged Potawatomi Trail. In this guide, we have described and covered more than 50 trails, from Pontiac and Pentwater to Grand Rapids and Grand Blanc. They range in difficulty, scenery and length and include short loops ideal for families and beginners. There are areas where you'll encounter more birdlife than bikers and rugged systems where the hills and narrow track challenges even the most seasoned mountain bikers.

But they are all routes that can be enjoyed on your fat-tire bike...and they are all in southern Michigan, close to home.

When To Ride

For some people mountain biking is a year-round sport. For others, it's something to enjoy only in July, but every cyclist should avoid riding too early in the spring. Multi-use trails are most susceptible to mountain bike erosion in late March and early April when spring break-up leaves the top soil soft and vulnerable.

Traditionally in southern Michigan trails are hard enough for mountain bike use by mid-April. But a long winter or extensive snow accumulation can alter that date by a week or more. The rule of thumb used by the Michigan Mountain Biking Association is ***don't ride the trails until the worms come up***. If no worms come up at night, then there is a wet layer of top soil covering frozen ground. Pedal a mountain bike across it and you'll separate the two layers and hasten the erosion of a trail bed.

Also be conscious of other users of public land. Don't ride in state game areas or recreation areas during the firearm deer season Nov. 15-30, when these tracts draw a large number of hunters. When there is three inches or more of snow on the ground, stay off trail systems that are popular with cross country skiers, such as Bald Mountain Recreation Area. You're not only infringing on their relatively short season in southern Michigan, but you're damaging what little snow they have to ski on.

Rules of the Trail

The International Mountain Bicycling Association has come up with six "Rules of the Trail" that all bikers should remember and follow:

1. Ride on open trails only. Respect trail and road closures, private property, and requirements for permits and authorization. Federal and state wilderness areas are closed to cycling, and some park and forest trails are also off limits, particularly those in the dune areas along Lake Michigan.

2. Leave no trace. Don't ride when the ground will be marred, such as on certain soils after a rain. Never ride off the trail, skid your tires, or discard any object. Strive to pack out more than you pack in.

3. Control your bicycle. Inattention for even a second can cause disaster. Excessive speed frightens and injures people, gives mountain biking a bad name, and results in trail closures.

4. Always yield the trail. Make your approach known well in advance. A friendly greeting is considerate and appreciated. Show your respect when passing others by slowing to walking speed or even stopping. Anticipate that other trail users may be around corners or in blind spots.

5. Never spook animals.

6. Plan ahead. Know your equipment, your ability, and the area in which you are riding and prepare accordingly.

Be self-sufficient at all times, keep your bike in good repair,

and carry necessary supplies for changes in weather. Keep trails open by setting an example of responsible cycling for all to see.

The Michigan Mountain Biking Association also has a Responsibility Code:

1. Always yield the right of way to other trail users
2. Slow down and pass with care (or stop)
3. Control your speed at all times
4. Stay on designated trails
5. Don't disturb wildlife or livestock
6. Pack out litter
7. Respect public and private property
8. Know local rules
9. Plan ahead
10. Minimize impact
11. Avoid riding in large groups
12. Report incidents of trail impasse to local authorities.

Trail Fees

State parks and recreation areas, as well as most county parks, charge a vehicle entry fee as a daily permit or an annual park pass. Some trails, most notably state forest pathways and national forest trails, maintain donation pipes at the trailheads.

Pay your fees. This is the era of "user pays" and if we want the trails open then we must toss a few dollars in the donation pipe.

Trail Difficulty

The Trail Difficulty rating used in this book is a way to indicate the physical exertion required to ride the route. It's influenced by the elevation gain (length and steepness) and technical difficulty of a ride, including width and character of the trail, obstacles (roots, sand, etc.), and length of technical sections.

Easy: This is a relatively flat ride with very little elevation gain along a fairly wide trail or two-track. Most easy trails feature few, if any, sharp turns while uphill portions are short and gentle.

Moderate: These trails include two-track, single track and often significant changes in elevation as well as short technical sections. They usually require more endurance than technical skill but you will encounter segments of tight and twisty single track. Most moderate trails in this guide can be handled by beginners if they are prepared to hop off their bike from time to time.

Strenuous: Advanced trails can be all single track and feature short steep climbs, mile-long ascents or both. Bikers should expect rocks, roots and logs on the trail. Although there are some short advanced trails, many are long rides that require the biker to be self-sufficient with bike tools, first aid kit, a map and possibly a compass if the area is laced with trails, two-tracks and forest roads.

What trail should you ride and what should you avoid? Keep in mind that an advanced biker is someone who can ride at least 15 miles and not get completely burned out, no matter the terrain. They can cover hills without hopping off the bike, brake without excessively skidding and manage trailside repairs.

On the other hand, some bikers maintain that anybody can do any trail as long as they are prepared to hop off their bike and walk a segment that is obviously too difficult. There is no shame and it's a lot safer to walk the technical segments of a any trail.

The important thing is to enjoy yourself and for beginners that usually means avoiding the strenuous trails and bypassing around technical sections. *Mountain Biking Michigan* will allow you to evaluate a trail in advance and then decide if you have the skill level to enjoy it, not just survive it. As your skills progress, you can begin tackling harder trails until you're riding with the best of them.

Finally, regardless of the trail difficulty, let others know where you are and when you expect to be back. This is especially true if you ride alone.

Michigan Mountain Biking Association

Michigan Mountain Biking Association is a statewide organization that was formed in 1990 to secure trail access for off-road bikers and to oversee a series of quality mountain biking races in Michigan. Today there are more than 1,000 members of MMBA and almost 30 bike shops that are MMBA sponsors.

Much of the maintenance and construction of mountain biking trails in Southern Michigan is done by volunteers of various MMBA chapters. The local chapter will adopt a trail system and then organize work parties and fund-raising events to keep the trails maintain.

To ensure the future of mountain biking in Michigan, join the MMBA and then become active in your local chapter. For an application form write to MMBA, 2526 Elizabeth Lake Rd., Waterford, MI 48328.

Biking Lingo

New to the sport of mountain biking? Here's some terms you might run across in this book, out on the trail or in a bike shop:

Aerodynamic position: The position the rider takes on the bike in order to let air flow over and around the body with as little interference as possible.

Bar ends: Horn-like fittings on the handlebars that are helpful in climbing.

Biff bucket: A biker's helmet. Also called a "skid lid."

Bonk: When a rider runs out of energy. Equivalent to a runner "hitting the wall."

Bottom bracket height: The distance from the ground to the center of the crank spindle. Low bottom brackets lend stabil-

One of the best times to mountain bike in southern Michigan is late September through October to enjoy fall colors and cool temperatures.

ity, high bottom brackets yield better cornering and ground clearance.

Bunny hop: Lifting the mountain bike while riding it. Being able to bunny hop can help a rider clear obstacles in the trail such as rocks, stumps, logs, and ruts.

Catching air: When a mountain biker hits a rise or drop-off in the trail and the bike is in the air momentarily. The rider must then be careful to keep the bike balanced to avoid landing off the trail.

Chain-ring: The crank arm rings that the chain rides on. A mountain bike can have as many as four chain-rings, but three is more common.

Chain-stay: The length of tube that connects the bottom bracket to the rear axle.

Clipless pedals: Shoe/pedal combinations that do not require toe-clips. The shoes mate with spring-loaded fittings on the pedals to provide more efficient transfer of power from the rider to the bike. The drawback is their high price compared to toe-clips.

Crank set: This includes the chain-rings and crank arm of the bike.

Derailleur: The device that moves the chain up or down on the chain-rings (the front derailleur), or up and down on the sprockets connected to the rear wheel (rear derailleur).

Endo: When a rider somersaults over the handlebars "end over end."

Face plant: A rider who just endured an endo.

Freewheel: A device attached to the rear wheel of a bicycle, permitting wheel motion without pedal action, i.e. coasting. A mountain bike can have as many as eight cogs on the freewheel, which allows the rider a wide range of gear choices.

Hardtail: A bike without rear suspension.

Knobbies: Mountain bike tires with aggressive, ground-holding tread patterns.

Quick-release: A device that allows for fast adjustment or release of the seat or wheels.

Single track: A trail only wide enough for one mountain bike. These trails are usually the most fun and challenging segments to ride.

Shorty levers (two-finger levers): The shape of a brake lever. They are shorter than traditional levers to avoid snagging on something while riding down a trail.

Stand-over height: The space a bicyclist has when standing over the top tube of the bike. A person should allow roughly three inches of clearance between the top tube of a mountain bike and the crotch area.

Suspension: A shock absorber to smooth out the ride. Front-suspension bikes have the shock absorber built into the front fork or headset; duel-suspension has them both in the front and rear.

Toe-clips: A plastic or metal band with a strap attached that secures the foot to the pedal for more power and better control.

Two-track: A trail wide enough for two or more bikers.

Wheelbase: The measurement between the front and rear axles. A long wheelbase can make a bike ride smoother; a short wheelbase can make a bike respond quicker when turning and handling.

Southeast Michigan

Holdridge Lakes Mountain Bike Area in Holly Recreation Area attracks a small number of riders throughout the winter.

Holdridge Lakes

County: Oakland
Total Mileage: 7 miles along five loops
Terrain: Low marshes and rolling hills
Fees: Annual state park pass or daily vehicle entry permit
Difficulty: Easy to moderate

Holdridge Lakes Mountain Biking Area was built by the Holly-Flint Chapter of MMBA whose members used overgrown equestrian trails in the Holly Recreation Area to form a 7-mile system. Opened in 1995, the trails are narrow, requiring plenty of squeeze-between-the-trees maneuvers. A very short Tech Loop from the Long Loop provides an additional steep climb and a couple of log jumps.

Riders need only basic technical skills to navigate the woodlands that include several small lakes and marshes. Except for some lowlying wet areas, most of trail bed is hard pack, composed of clay amalgamate. Floating bridges and trail mats have been used to stabilize the trail in the areas around marshes.

The scenery is pleasant and the terrain makes for an interesting blend of turns. But be forewarned: all that standing water in the marshes is nothing short of a bug factory, especially from mid-June through July. On this system you need repellent, not sun screen, as there are far more bugs here than open areas for the sun to shine down on you.

The only facilities at the trailhead are a pair of vault toilets. Bring your own water.

Getting There: From I-75, 19 miles north of Pontiac, depart at exit 101 and head west onto Grange Hall Road. Immediately turn north on Hess Road and the posted parking lot and trailhead is reached in 1.5 miles.

Information: Contact Holly Recreation Area, 8100 Grange Hall Road, Holly, MI 48442; ☎ (810) 634-8811.

Long Loop

Distance: 4 miles
Trail: Single track
Direction: Clockwise

From the parking lot, all the south loops begin along the All Trails stretch, a narrow track that winds through a series of small hills. Within a third of a mile you reach the intersection with the Short Loop. Head left to stay on the Long Loop that is initially strewn with rocks as it skirts a lowlying forested area.

This first mile is damp and bumpy and requires a bit of bike balance to negotiate the scattering of wet roots and stones. This section is scenic throughout the year but especially during winter rides when the snow is sparkling along the trail. The track then winds through the swale, close enough to the marshes at **Mile 1.2** to offer some interesting scenery if the deer flies aren't chasing you. Unfortunately there are also enough roots and tight turns through trees to keep most eyes on the trail.

You climb out of the lowlands to a somewhat dry stretch in the woods where the trail weaves among the numerous marshes.

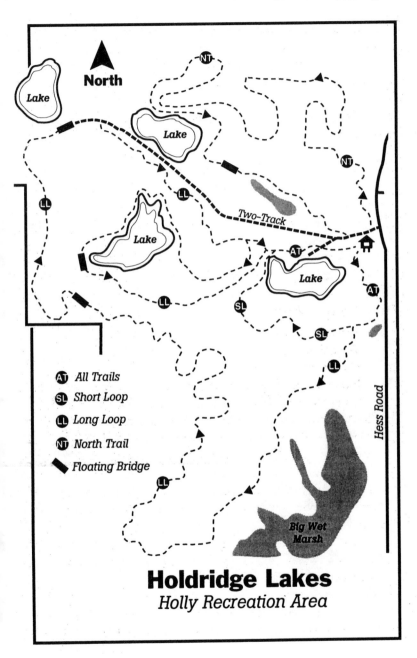

Holdridge Lakes
Holly Recreation Area

Legend:
- **AT** All Trails
- **SL** Short Loop
- **LL** Long Loop
- **NT** North Trail
- Floating Bridge

The trail climbs and descends a ridge repeatedly. The trees are close together in this stretch of track, which also includes a couple of slippery log crossings before descending into a sometimes sloppy lowlying area.

At **Mile 2**, halfway around the Long Loop, there are floating bridges and trail mat that help stabilize the wet trail bed. Within a third of a mile, there is a bridge followed immediately by a short off-camber climb along a ridge. You descend to a swamp and then are faced with the "Steep Hill" noted on the trail map. This hill is a little bit rude and has roots at the top, but also a bench so you can catch your breath while watching others struggle with the climb.

From here you climb again to higher, dry ground in the rolling woods that leads to the intersection with the short Tech Loop at **Mile 3.3**.

The Tech Loop is 0.2-mile long spur that provides an additional descent and climb. It joins the Long Loop, where you immediately cross a bridge, climb a small hill and then roll along a two track briefly.

The Long Loop splits off, returns to a wooded setting and at **Mile 3.5** reaches the junction with the Short Cut, which quickly returns to the trailhead. The Long Loop heads south (right) and skirts a marshy lake adding a scenic half mile. You first encounter Paul's Slide, a short but rocky descent and then reach the lake, where at the north end is a bench and an open view of the water. Look for the blue herons that hang out here much of the summer.

You skirt the backside of the lake and then pass through a lowlying area with floating bridges and trail mats. Eventually the Long Loop returns to Short Cut and heads east (right) into the parking lot.

Short Loop

Distance: 0.6 mile
Trail: Single track
Direction: Clockwise
This is a short and easy trail, ideal for beginners. Start with

the All Trails stretch that is described above and then make a right at the first intersection. Initially there are some lowlands on this trail so floating bridges have been installed. The ride stays low and flat and skirts a little lake before merging with the return stretch of the All Trails section. Turn right here, cross a bridge and follow the two track to the parking lot.

North Loop

Distance: 2 miles
Trail: Single track
Direction: Counter clockwise

This is the newest loop of the Holdridge Lakes Mountain Bike Area, opened in the fall of 1995. It is rated easy to moderate because of the handful of stumps that will remain until the trail bed wears in. The first quarter mile is a little roller coaster ride through the woods until the trail pops out into a field. You wander along the fields until **Mile 1**, where the trail dips back into the woods briefly and then winds through some swale.

At **Mile 1.7** there is a huge tree followed by a short and narrow bridge. The rest of the ride is a mixture of open fields and brief stretches through the trees until you return to the parking lot at **Mile 2**.

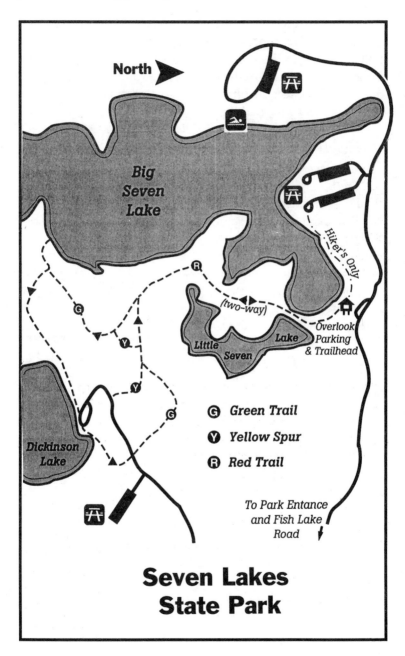

North

Big
Seven
Lake

R

(two-way)

G

Y

Little   Lake

Seven

Hiker's Only

Overlook
Parking
& Trailhead

Y

G

Dickinson
Lake

G Green Trail

Y Yellow Spur

R Red Trail

To Park Entrance
and Fish Lake
Road

Seven Lakes
State Park

Seven Lakes State Park

County: Oakland
Total Mileage: 3.4 miles
Terrain: Rolling hills, fields and lakes
Fees: Annual state park pass or daily vehicle entry permit
Difficulty: Easy to moderate

Seven Lakes State Park has a lightly used system that offers beginners and families a short but fun ride. There is potential to expand here and someday this 1,400-acre park may develop a trail system that not only increases its mileage but also includes some technical sections.

The park has three lakes near the trails, while its largest, Big Seven Lake, features a beach and picnic area. You'll find restrooms and water at both the beach, Dickinson Shelter and in the campground.

The Overlook Parking Lot is the best place to start. To reach it from the contact station continue west, passing the campground road. A Red connector trail is down the slope, east of the parking lot, and leads to the Red/Green Loop. The Red Trail to the west is for hikers only.

Getting There: The park is just south of Flint. From I-75, depart at exit 101 and head west on Grange Hall Road past Holly. Turn north on Fish Lake Road where and the entrance will be reached in a mile.

Information: Contact Seven Lakes State Park, 2220 Tinsman Rd., Fenton MI 48430; ☎ (810) 634-7271.

Red\Green Trail

Distance: 3.2 miles
Trail: Single track
Direction: Two way on the Red connector; counter-clockwise on the Green Loop

From the Overlook parking lot, descend towards the lake and then head left at the sign for the Red Trail. The trail starts in a grassy field but quickly enters a forest and follows a narrow, winding course among the trees. The hills along this stretch are very short, steep and close together for a fun ride.

At **Mile 0.4** a spur on the right leads to the lake for fishing access. At this point the trail climbs away from the lake into the forest to intersect the Yellow Trail. This is a shortcut back to the parking lot, but can be used to form a figure-eight to give the rider additional loop combinations.

Heading right, the Green Trail becomes less technical and passes another spur to the lake at **Mile 1**. From here the trail becomes progressively tamer. It passes through a field as it skirts Dickinson Lake and then crosses the park road. Pick up the trail on the other side as it briefly dips back into the woods.

The Green Trail passes a set of stairs and a foot path and then winds through the woods on a two-track. You climb out of the lake bowl and into a picnic area with vault toilets and water at **Mile 2**. The trail is difficult to see here but easy to pick up after it crosses the park road.

Crossing back into the woods again the Green Trail threads through the woods and intersects a short cut to the picnic area.

Seven Lakes State Park features a limited trail system that is ideal for families and novice riders.

Stay right and right again as the Green Trail returns to the Yellow Trail at **Mile 2.4**.

The final stretch of trail is another run through those favorite rolling hills to meet the Red Trail at **Mile 2.8**. Head right and remember this trail is used for outbound bike traffic as well as by hikers and anglers. At **Mile 3.2**, you arrive at the Overlook Parking Lot.

A mountain biker pauses near one of the trailheads of the North Unit in Bald Mountain Recreation Area. The state park unit features more than 15 miles of trails that are open to mountain bikers.

Bald Mountain Recreation Area

County: Oakland
Total Mileage: 15 miles
Terrain: Wooded, rolling hills and lakes
Fees: Daily vehicle entry permit or annual state park Pass
Difficulty: Easy to moderate

You want to ride the most challenging mountain bike trail system in Oakland County? Head west to Pontiac Lake Recreation Area. You want to enjoy the most scenic ride in the county? Then head north to Bald Mountain Recreation Area, where the trails wind around a dozen small lakes, past marshy ponds and over gurgling Spring Creek.

Located just east of Lake Orion, this **4637-acre** state park unit offers the most extensive collection of trails in Southeast Michigan. Its North Unit, just north of Stoney Creek Road, contains four loops that total **8** miles; its South Unit, accessed from Greenshield Road, is a 7-mile figure eight loop. Passing between the two units is the Paint Creek Rail Trail, a crushed slag route that spans 10 miles from Lake Orion to Rochester along the bed of a former railroad.

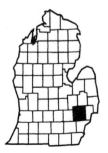

Both units feature the same type of forest

cover and a rolling terrain while the South Unit tends to skirt a number of ponds, marshes and low lying wet areas. The trail here can be wet and mushy, especially before mid-May. This makes the North Unit more popular among mountain bikers. In general, its trail system remains dry as it weaves around many small lakes, including Prince, Chamberlain, and East and West Graham Lakes. The North Unit also sports clusters of rolling hills; even one with a bench and excellent view of West Graham Lake.

Bald Mountain lies in something of minor snowbelt in Oakland County. When there is sufficient snow in January and February skiers flock to the North Unit trails while snowmobilers are allowed in the South Unit. If not, then a tickle of hard-core mountain bikers are on the trails almost every weekend throughout the winter. Keep in mind the park is open to deer hunting in November while April and early May is usually to wet and vulnerable to the erosion damage of mountain bikes.

Getting There: To reach the North Unit from I-75 depart at exit 81 and head north on M-24 6 miles to Clarkston Road. Head east on Clarkston Road, a scenic dirt road, and follow it carefully as it jogs to the left over Paint Creek and passes a trailhead for the Paint Creek Rail-Trail. This can be a confusing corner. Turn north on Adams Road which ends at Stoney Creek Road. Turn east on Stoney Creek Road briefly and then north on Harmon Road. Follow Harmon a half mile to the junction with Predmore Road where there are two parking lots. The western one has a trailhead that makes for smoother access and avoids the congestion of two-way trail traffic.

To reach the South Unit depart M-24 at Greenshield Road and head east a half mile to a parking area on the north side of the road. Further east on Greenshield is the park headquarters, open Monday through Friday from 8 a.m. to 5 p.m.

Information: Contact Bald Mountain Recreation Area, 1330 Greenshield, Rt. 1, Lake Orion, MI 48360, ☎ (810) 693-6767.

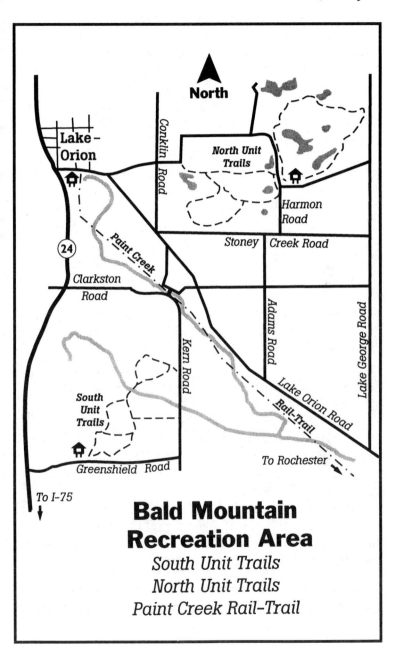

North

Lake-Orion

Conklin Road

North Unit Trails

Harmon Road

(24)

Paint Creek

Stoney Creek Road

Clarkston Road

Kern Road

Adams Road

Lake George Road

South Unit Trails

Lake Orion Road

Rail-Trail

Greenshield Road

To Rochester

To I-75

Bald Mountain
Recreation Area
South Unit Trails
North Unit Trails
Paint Creek Rail-Trail

North Unit Trails

Distance: 6.8 miles
Trail: Single track
Direction: Clockwise

This ride follows the outside trails of the North Unit for a 6.8-mile loop. From the trailhead near Heart Lake head south along the shore to Post 2, a junction with the Green connector loop. Stay right at the post as the trail passes the Tamarack Lake Cabins on the left, the site of vault toilets and a seasonal water pump.

Beyond the cabins, you continue in the woods, climb a hill and then pass a couple of unsanctioned spurs. Stay on the main trail until you reach Post 3 at the split of the Blue and White loops. Turn right to stay on the White trail and shorten the ride by a half mile. Head left and you climb up the Blue Loop towards the sledding hill.

Near **Mile 0.5**, you are at the top of a small gully and rolling across an intersection with more unsanctioned spurs. Beyond these spurs is a second gully with loose rocks that can be wet and muddy during spring. The Blue Loop then climbs the sledding hill and just prior to reaching the top you arrive at three spurs. The right spur is a bypass and leads past the east edge of Carpenter Lake. The center and left spurs circumvent the crest of the hill. The left spur is a steep descent on a loose and rutted trail with deep washouts. Beginners should avoid this spur.

From the sledding hill, the Blue Loop moves into rolling hills and passes the west edge of Carpenter Lake and then the north side, where there are a couple of muddy areas with floating bridges and cedar chips. The surrounding marshes produce enough mosquitoes so that in the summer this is not a good place to be repairing a flat tire.

Just past **Mile 1** there is a half-mile stretch of moderate, rolling hills, not steep but great fun. At **Mile 1.7** you pass the sledding hill bypass and then quickly reach Post 5, the intersection with the White Loop. There is a bench at this marker.

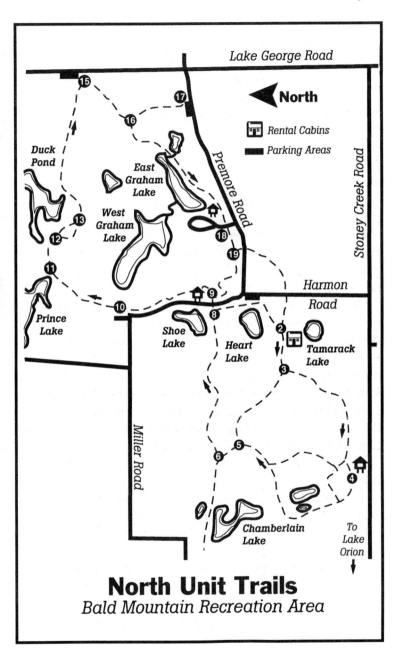

North Unit Trails
Bald Mountain Recreation Area

Stay left to continue on the White Loop heading north and then turn right at Post 6. The trail moves up a rise followed by a fast little downhill segment that narrows and becomes deep sand at the bottom. Use caution on this hill.

From here the trail swings left around Shoe Lake and reaches Harmon Road just before *Mile 3.8*. Use caution as you approach the road since this is a short piece of two-way trail that does not have good visibility.

After crossing the road, the trail immediately reaches Post 9, where you turn left to stay on the outside loop along the Orange segment. Here the trail heads north and climbs the best hill. On the way up, you pass a view of Shoe Lake and then pop out at the top where there is a view of West Graham Lake and the surrounding ridges. You then descend to skirt along Harmon Road through a soft, loose trail. Near *Mile 4.3* there is a parking lot at Post 10, although the actual post itself might be gone.

Continue north to Prince Lake and Post 11. Post 12 is near the top of a small rise where the trail splits into two short pieces that rejoin quickly at Post 13. Staying right gives you a roller coaster sensation from a fast downhill and uphill then a sharp right turn to the post at the top.

The next quarter mile is mostly a downhill run, followed by a gentle climb to Post 14 at *Mile 5.6*. Post 15 is reached within a third of a mile and serves as a trailhead for a parking area off Lake George Road. Follow the trail as it bends right and you emerge on a fast, hilly run that some bikers nicked-named "the screaming beamies."

On this stretch there is a fast descent and a sharp right turn obstructed by brush that will catch you off guard if you're going too fast. At Post 16, stay right. The other spur heads south to a trailhead and parking area on Predmore Road.

After passing Post 16, the main trail continues as rolling single track until *Mile 6.2*, where it crosses a bridge over a stream that flows from Dorn Lake to East Graham Lake. The bridge makes a nice place to enjoy the wetland scenery, but be aware of any oncoming traffic.

At **Mile 6.5** you roll up to Post 18 and the access road to a parking area off Predmore Road. At this trailhead area there is a boat launch and a small fishing pier on East Graham Lake. Slow your approach to this access road as the surrounding the scrub growth makes seeing and hearing traffic difficult.

Post 19 marks the intersection with The Green connector loop running south (left) across Predmore and then Harmon Roads to join the White Loop at Post 2. If you go right at Post 19 the last tenth of a mile returns you to Post 9 and the parking lot. The combination of two-way trail traffic and road crossings make caution necessary for either choice. By beginning and ending at Post 9, you have the advantage of adding another ride along either the White, Blue or Orange loops for additional mileage.

South Unit Trails

Distance: 4.8 miles
Trail: Single track
Direction: Clockwise

The main South Unit trailhead is one mile east of M-24 off Greenshield Road, on the north side. Mountain bikers on the Paint Creek Trail, however, will depart the rail trail where it crosses Clarkston Road and head south on Kern Road. Within a mile you can enter the park at group campground and pick up the South Unit trail system at its north end.

From the parking lot head out on the Red Trail through an open field towards Post 2 where you will head left. The single-track continues through low brush and sapling woods, passing a marshy pond and at **Mile 0.8** reaching Post 3. This is the junction with the Orange crossover spur and turning right shortens the outing to a 2.5-mile ride.

Stay left at Post 3 and within a half mile you will pass a large pond surrounded by farm fields on the far side. This segment has a few rolling hills and some lowlying wet areas that the park staff has filled with stone to combat erosion. At Post 4, you move

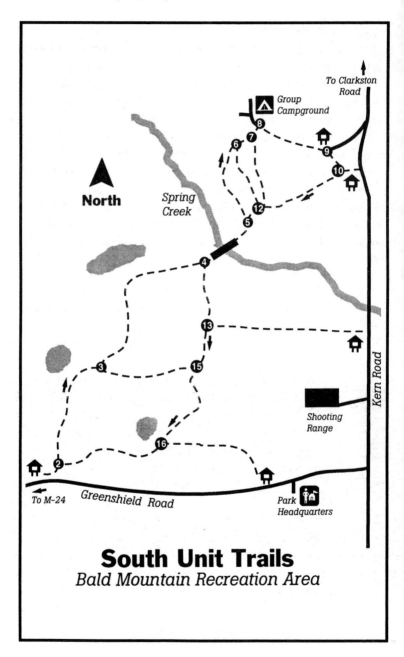

South Unit Trails
Bald Mountain Recreation Area

onto a two-way trail that gently descends to cross Spring Creek via a bridge. On the other side the trail climbs steeply along a ridgeline that passes another pothole marsh before arriving at Post 5 near **Mile 2**. The climb is the most significant of the route, although the hill is still only moderately challenging.

Turn left at Post 5 as the trail descends past the pothole marsh then climbs again to Post 6. This marker and Post 7, just up the trail, offer right turn options that are crossover spurs. The first is the Green Trail, a wet ride; the second is the Blue Trail that follows higher ground between bogs.

Post 8 at **Mile 2.4** is the intersection with a spur coming from the group campground. If you need water you can turn left and head for the campground parking area where there is a seasonal water pump. If you want to add additional mileage, head north from the campground on Kern Road and in a mile you'll intersect Paint Creek Trail, a crushed slag rail trail.

To stay on the outside loop make a right at Post 8, where the trail becomes a two-track as it joins the group campground access road from Kern Road. At the next two trail markers, Post 9 and Post 10, turn right to bypass spurs to Kern Road.

The trail returns to being a single track and then passes the junctions of the Blue and Green crossover spurs. Stay left to return to Post 5, where you descend the hill to Spring Creek. *Be alert for oncoming traffic before crossing the bridge at the bottom.* On the other side is Post 4, where you turn left.

A stone-filled section through a wet area follows and is loose enough to make navigation a challenge. At Post 13 there is a wide access trail on the left leading out to Kern Road. Head right here and be prepared for more wet trail. When you reach Post 15, continue left and then right at Post 16 to reach the trailhead. A left at Post 16 would take you to the park office. Remember that heading left at Post 2 puts you on a two-way trail for the parking lot. Ride this segment with regard for outbound hikers and bikers.

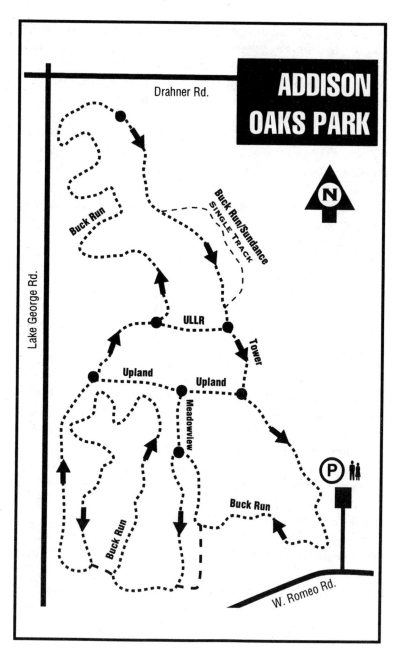

Addison Oaks County Park

County: Oakland
Total Mileage: 5 miles
Terrain: Flat with mixture of fields and woods
Fees: A vehicle entry fee into the park
Difficulty: Easy to moderate

Addison Oaks was a bit of a trial balloon for the Oakland County Parks Department. A picturesque area, the park initially provided mountain biking opportunities on its already established cross country ski trails but recently the staff has added some single track. This new pieces, the only stretches rated moderate in difficulty, are short, gnarly, tight, and filled with technical turns.

Park managers are committed to re-routing the course so the single track will continue to change. Be on your toes if you ride the new segments as they can be surprisingly challenging and are recommended for experienced bikers. The rest of the trail system in this 794-acre park moves through established woods and open fields and is an easy ride that can be handled by most beginners and families.

Park facilities include restrooms and water in the concessions building near the parking area. There are also toilets at the southwest corner of Lake Buhl near the Lakefront Pavilion and directly north of Lake Buhl in the primitive camping area.

Getting There: From I-75 depart at exit 81 and head north on M-24. Just before entering Lake Orion, turn east on Clarkston Road and follow it as it winds through a section of Bald Mountain Recreation Area. Turn north on Lake George Road for a half mile to Predmore Road, where you turn east (right). Turn north (left) on Kline Road and follow it as it takes you pass Romeo Road right into the park entrance.

To reach the trailhead from the parking area, ride towards the park entrance and then head due west at the contact station instead of following the drive.

Information: Contact Addison Oaks, 1480 West Romeo, Leonard MI 48367-8305; ☎ (810) 693-2432. Or call the Oakland County Parks Department at ☎ (810) 858-0906.

Buck Run

Distance: 4.3 miles
Trail: Two-track and some single track
Direction: Clockwise

From the trailhead, head right to start the ride with a short flat stretch followed by a climb to the top of the water tower hill. The trail then becomes its characteristic run through woods and fields. You quickly pass a service road on the left and a corn field on the right and then at **Mile 0.5** Buck Run passes a shortcut on the right called Meadowview.

Stay left to remain on Buck Run which winds into the most scenic forested section of the trail system. Near **Mile 1** the service road reappears on the left while Buck Run heads right to pass through a stand of oaks and maples. The service road pops up a third time near **Mile 2**. Head right as Buck Run rolls through the forest to emerge from the trees at the Upland Trail.

Stay left at the Upland intersection and again at ULLR, at **Mile**

Some of the earliest mountain bike races in the state were staged at Addison Oaks, a unit of the Oakland County park system.

2.5. Buck Run then meanders through corn fields, woods and meadows to arrive at a bench at the north end of the trail system at **Mile 3.4**. From here it is only a quarter mile to the original single track seen on the left.

This short track is technical but fun as it rolls in and out of a natural bowl. During late autumn, when there are leaves on the ground, the trail is elusive as flits in and out of sight. The forest is dense here and it's possible at times to ride past deer unaccustomed to bikes. The last half of the single track climbs to meet the regular trail near the water tower.

Those wanting to bypass the single track can continue straight at the intersection with it and head along the final stretch towards the water tower. From the tower it's a sweet descent through the woods that provides a kinetic push back to the car.

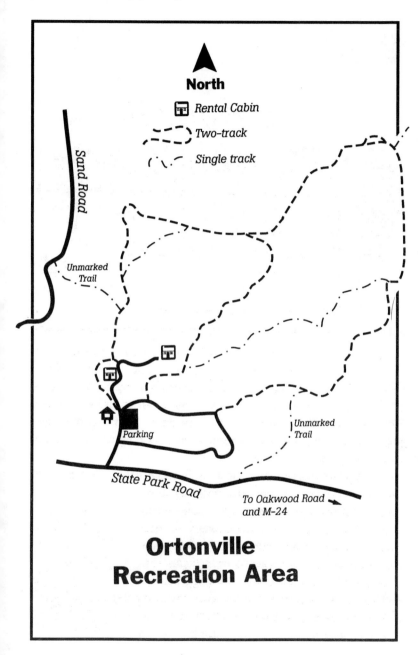

North

🏠 *Rental Cabin*

Two-track

Single track

Sand Road

Unmarked Trail

Unmarked Trail

Parking

State Park Road

To Oakwood Road and M-24 →

Ortonville Recreation Area

Ortonville Recreation Area

County: Oakland
Total Mileage: 5 miles.
Terrain: Hilly with moderate sand
Fees: Daily vehicle entry permit or annual state park pass
Difficulty: Easy to moderate

This tremendous but little used trail is a small system at the southern end of the Ortonville Recreation Area, just north of the town of Ortonville. The trail has few signs marking its many intersections and what is present are carryovers from its original use as a hiking system. The signs are oriented to be seen when approached counter clockwise but judicious viewing of the map on preliminary visits is a must.

Biking the outside loop in a clockwise direction will provide you with a woodland route broken up by semi-open fields filled with crab apple, chokecherry and at times a variety of wild flowers. At least on the first lap! After getting a lay of the land on one loop, exploring inside forks is highly recommended, which includes a technical section in the lower western corner that requires mountain biking experience. There are also

some sobering descents on the outside loop near the end.

Overall the trail system is somewhat short and generally not difficult. But Ortonville is visually delightful and provides enough bike handling and loop combinations to make up for its lack of mileage and keep most riders happy.

Be aware that Poison Ivy is prevalent in many sections of this system. By wearing tights or tall socks, you should be able to avoid the harmful effects of this non-climbing variety.

Getting There: The recreation area is halfway between M-24 and I-75, 20 miles north of Pontiac. From I-75, depart at exit 91 and head 8 miles north on M-15 to Oakwood Road just north of the town of Ortonville. Head east (right) on Oakwood Road for a mile and then north (left) on Sands Road. In less than a mile head east (right) on State Park Road and watch for the *Bloomer No. 3 Ortonville Recreation Area* sign on the left that marks the parking area.

Information: Contact Ortonville Recreation Area, 5779 Hadley Rd, Rt.2, Ortonville, MI 48462; ☎ (810) 627-3828

Outside Loop
Distance: 3.8 miles
Trail: Single track and two-track
Direction: Clockwise recommended
From the parking area head left around the water pump and begin on the two-track that leads to the rental cabins. The trail immediately veers left and climbs a ridge overlooking a cabin. You quickly reach a second junction where you veer left again to follow a trail around the cabins. This trails moves through flowering fields as it climbs slowly into the woods. You soon discover the trail is usually more sandy in the open fields than in the woods.

At **Mile 1**, the trail dips into the crab apple trees that rain petals on you in late spring. You reach a junction at **Mile 1.7** where the trail climbs to the right into the filtered shade of mixed deciduous trees. This climb lingers almost to **Mile 2**.

Here you head northeast to a connector loop, reached at **Mile 2**. The connector loop shoots to the south (right) and takes you back to the parking lot. By staying left, the trail continues in a mixture of rolling woods and open fields.

At **Mile 2.3** there is a unmarked spur that leads north to Sawmill Lake Road. The main trail heads south through some over-grown honeysuckle and into an area of deep woods, wild fruit trees and meadows.

Near **Mile 3** the trail climbs to where there is a junction with the narrow technical spur. The main trail heads left (south) down a steep descent while the spur is a challenging single track that includes much twisting along a ridge. The spur then runs out into semi-open meadow along the side of a hill before making a easy but surprisingly steep downhill run. It finishes with a technical rock-and-roll ride where it joins a two-track that races downhill into the parking area.

The main trail bypasses this technical piece by cutting south through rolling hills of dense forest. Another unmarked spur is reached at **Mile 3.2** that leads left (south) to State Park Road. This spur is not recommended for beginners or intermediate riders as it includes a challenging descent along washboard-like trail.

The main trail, on the other hand, puts you on a thrilling descent of sand and roots that rolls onto a two-track at **Mile 3.4**. Stay left where the trail splits and ride the final leg, another fast descent, into the parking lot, reached at **Mile 3.8**.

The trail system at Pontiac Lake Recreation Area is a challenging ride in which mountain bikers must be sure their bike is mechanically in top form before starting out.

Pontiac Lake Recreation Area

County: Oakland
Total Mileage: 11.5 miles
Terrain: Forested hills and fields
Fees: Daily vehicle entry permit or annual state park pass
Difficulty: Moderate to strenuous

Pontiac Lake Recreation Area is a 3,700-acre state park unit with a wide variety of terrain, several overlooks on hills and ridges and a popular mountain bike trail winding through the center of it. This trail is so popular that on the weekends it is often packed with bike traffic by mid-morning.

But be forewarned: the route is noted for its roots and rocks. Most riders will find the network challenging in its obstacles and speed. Pay attention or such obstacles can hurt you. There are several notable climbs; some are steep, some are loose and some are both loose and steep. Some of the hills have earned nicknames, like Little Puke, so time your pre-ride meals.

Within the park is a horse stable and occasionally the bike trail intersect equestrian trails, which are off limits to bikers. Many bikers use the trails year round while the park hosts mountain bike events during the summer.

Getting There: From Pontiac head west on M-59 (Highland Road) and turn north onto Williams Lake Road. Turn west onto Gale Road and follow it for a mile to the posted dayuse area and beach on Pontiac Lake. Head to the northwest corner of the parking lot where you will find the trailhead and display map.

Information: Contact Pontiac Lakes Recreation Area, 7800 Gale Road, Waterford, MI 48327; ☎ (810) 666-1020.

Outside Loop

Distance: 10.5 miles
Trail: Single track
Direction: Clockwise

From the parking lot the trail immediately crosses Gale Road, *where you need to be careful as frequently there is vehicle traffic.* On the north side of Gale Road the trail resumes as a two-track and continues for about a quarter of a mile before reaching a "Y" intersection and the starting marker. Head left to ride clockwise.

The two-track quickly becomes a single track as the trail heads for the woods and begins its signature roly-poly nature. It's a little off camber in places and then flattens out at **Mile 0.8** before drifting into deep sand as it climbs to an overlook. Before reaching the top you move through some pines along a loose section of trail that is deeply dished.

The crest of the overlook is reached at **Mile 1** where the trail crosses an equestrian trail. Watch for horses as you pop out of the woods quickly here. The descent on the backside is bumpy, fast and tricky with an off-camber, sharp and washed-out turn to the left. Keep things reined in. You are still in the woods and there are some rough sections with deep sand. At **Mile 1.7** the trail becomes more gentle and rolling and then makes a sweeping right-hand turn through all kinds of roots.

There are now two ways to climb to the overlook above the campground. The original route rises in tiers beginning on solid rock then moving into loose gravel and finally sand as the it winds to the left before topping out at **Mile 2**.

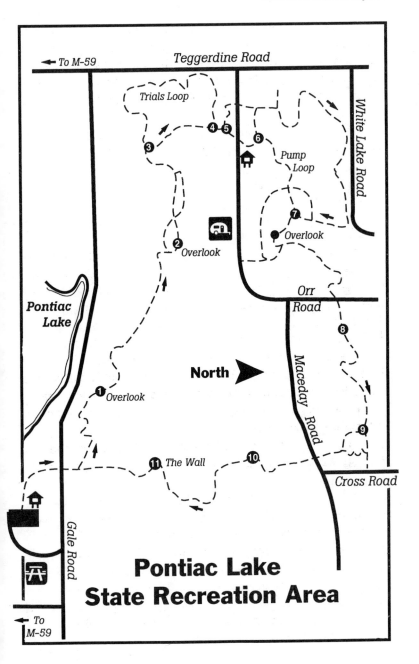

The descent from this overlook along the old route is treacherous! You barrel straight down and then make a gentle right but there is no resting here. You're immediately back on a rocket ride between pines before hitting some loose rocks at the bottom. Still racing, you fly into a left turn that opens into an ugly, wide, washed out descent, where many careless riders have gotten fractures.

To bypass the nasty descent use the left turn when ascending the campground hill at the second tier. Nicknamed Criss Cross, this trail climbs the hill, starts its descent and crosses the original trail. Be careful, because riders coming down the old route are moving really fast at this point. Criss Cross moves through a pine plantation and then rejoins the original trail. Again be cautious of speeding bikers on the other route here.

At **Mile 2.4** you reach the junction with the Trials Loop and will be moving fast. Make a right to bypass this loop and reduce the ride by a mile. Stay left to enter the loop, a concentration of challenges, entirely in the woods and generally saturated with roots. The wildness picks up just after **Mile 3** where you enter *The Rock Garden*. This is a jumpy assortment of mineral hazards followed by two notable climbs. The first is the fondly named *Little Puke*. Passing that will take you to *Big Puke*. The last challenge is where you torpedo downhill on a dished-out drainage called the *Toboggan Run* and finally rejoin the bypass just before **Mile 4**.

After a brief stretch, the trail forks just before crossing Maceday Road. To the left the trail heads north a quarter mile and arrives at another fork. Go right here to reach a water pump and ultimately the parking lot for the group campground.

Staying left at the pump bypass is considered the main loop. This section is a little bit of a roller coaster where you can carry speed to top of the climb near **Mile 4.5**, where there is an intersection. Stay to the right and the next 2 miles should maintain your interest though this stretch is not as challenging as the Trials Loop.

The trail curves through the woods where you encounter a two-foot drop and a stretch of jarring washboard that rattles you into a hard left turn. Near **Mile 5.5**, the trail crosses a field and passes an access trail. The spur is from a parking lot off White Lake Road, which is used primarily for people to reach a model airplane field just south of the bike trail.

After a sweeping right turn, the main trail passes a new spur to the right prior to intersecting the water pump bypass. By following this new trail to the right, you can continue south across the pump bypass and use a softer climb to a major overlook. This is the best option as the trail skirts the backside of the overlook for a slower and better descent as well. The descent off this overlook along the original trail is a badly eroded stretch at a steep angle. It's high speed to the bottom, where you'll encounter more loose rubble and low hanging branches.

Either way, you finish the hill by shooting into the forest and then riding through a delightful series of fast S-curves that end at Orr Road. The trail resumes on the other side of the road and at **Mile 7.7** reaches a noticeable intersection of four spurs. Make a left turn and follow the main trail.

There are more rocky climbs and bumpy downhill sections in this stretch, especially at **Mile 8.3** where the main trail swings south (right) with a fast descent. Staying left here will put you on a wide trail to Cross Road. Just before reaching the road, you intersect *Panty Ridge*, a twisty but fun single track that loops back to the main trail. You then descend a hill on the main trail before crossing Maceday Road for the second time. This portion of the road is closed to vehicle traffic.

At **Mile 8.6**, the trail moves through a stand of pines on its way to an intimidating climb called *The Wall*, reached at **Mile 9.3**. To bypass The Wall's steepest approach, follow the mowed path to the right for a more gentle climb to the top.

At the top of The Wall, the trail takes you briefly into the woods at **Mile 9.7** and then begins a rutted descent to the two-track that returns to the trailhead.

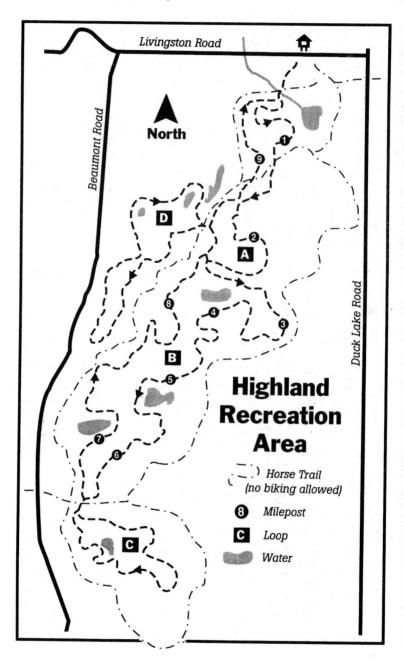

Livingston Road

Beaumont Road

North

Duck Lake Road

Highland Recreation Area

Horse Trail
(no biking allowed)

Milepost

Loop

Water

Highland Recreation Area

County: Oakland
Total Mileage: 16 miles
Terrain: Wooded, very hilly.
Fees: Annual state park sticker or daily vehicle entry permit.
Difficulty: Strenuous

Mountain bike history at Highland Recreation Area began in 1994 with the transformation of unused horse trails into a new trail system. Separated from the equestrian routes, this system was designed around the park's interesting terrain to produce challenging, enjoyable riding. But keep in mind; *the trails are very technical in an area where nothing is flat!*

The trail runs narrowly between trees and has many stretches of off-camber work guaranteed to keep your attention. Loop A is less than 4 miles long and is the shortest work-out. The trail is a delightful twist, requiring that you keep your speed in check and dance your way through it.

Many ponds line the trail. Some are scenic, others look like insect factories for the unprepared. The trail doesn't allow speed and it's hard to average more than 8 mph on it. Horse flies and other biting insects can be felt at that speed if you've forgotten repellent. Once used as pastures for livestock, the trail is littered with rock cairns and stone fences along with ant hills of similar heights. The B Loop is somewhat less twisty and gives the rider a wee bit of a rest until it rejoins A Loop. Loops C and D are both a workout with the D Loop now refered by many mountain bikers as "the hardest four miles of trail in Michigan."

Because most of this system is in the woods, sunscreen isn't needed while the thick canopy makes this trail system a good choice for rainy days or winter rides.

All trails are accessed directly from a single trailhead located across from the parking lot. At the trailhead are vault toilets but no source of water so bring plenty of liquids.

Highland Recreation Area also has picnic areas, campgrounds, a beach, and boat launch at areas away from the mountain biking trailhead. Practically across M-59 is the mountain bike system at Pontiac Lake Recreation Area.

Getting There: From M-59, 2 miles east of Milford Road, turn south on Duck Lake Road and then in a mile turn right at the first intersection onto Livingston Road. The trailhead and parking area will be reached in less than a quarter mile. The park headquarters is located off of M-59 east of the mountain bike trails between Ormond and Ford roads.

Information: Contact Highland Recreation Area, 5200 E. Highland Rd., Milford, MI 48042; ☎ (810) 685-2433.

Loop A
Distance: 3.8 miles
Trail: Narrow single track
Direction: Clockwise

The trail moves immediately into the woods and all mountain bike traffic shares the first stretch of track along with equestrians. *Watch for traffic here!* Within a few hundred yards, after the

The trail system at Highland Recreation Area has been enlarged to four loops and is now one of the most challenging rides for mountain bikers in southern Michigan.

stream crossing, horses veer right, mountain bikers left while the center trail is the return loop for cyclists.

From here Loop A becomes a lovely, winding, somewhat off-camber twist through the woods. Moving through the trees, the trail climbs a ridge with a marsh on the left. Indian Peace Pipes can be seen in mid-summer along this section.

Maximum alertness is required as you ride the twists to **Mile** *1*. The bike trail then crosses the equestrian trail (do not turn onto it) and resumes on the opposite side. Turning and twisting through the technical layout, you rocket through the sumac and near **Mile 2** ride past a pond of lily pads and hungry loosestrife.

The trail rolls between sections of a huge fallen tree, demonstrating how the designers kept the track narrow while leaving the terrain natural. A bench at the top of a rise welcomes bikers to rest before dropping down to pond level. At **Mile 2.25** the trail loops east around another pond before turning west and meeting the cutoff for the Loop B at **Mile 2.6**. Loop A stays right at the two B Loop intersections before descending into the dark woods where you have to dodge ground squirrel holes.

Near **Mile 2.8** is the D Loop spur, stay right and the horse trail will be visible 10 feet away on the left. Riding into the woods, at **Mile 3** you cross the horse trail and onto a bit of off-camber climbing along a ridgeline.

An open meadow leads you into the last stand of trees before you intersect the outbound trail at the stream crossing and return to the parking lot.

Loop B

Distance: 4.5 miles
Trail: Narrow single track
Direction: Clockwise

This loop is accessed at the halfway point of the Loop A and continues the crazy dance between trees. From A Loop turn left on Loop B and head south through the same kind of tight turns experienced earlier in the ride. The first stretch takes you out and back along a looping circuit that is best described as the fettuccine style of trail design; boiled fettuccine is dropped on a topographical map and voila! This is all great fun but not for the faint of heart.

The trail straightens out after more than a mile of this and wanders south, still testing your balance. Ultimately it swings around north again and (though hard to imagine!) offers higher density off-camber work as you close in on the junction with

Loop A. Picking a perfect line is a good objective here as there are a few rocket rides that must be done in full control or amorous trees will leave their mark.

The trail eventually merges into Loop A and bikers follow this loop that was described earlier. You can either return to the trailhead and parking lot or head out on Loop A again at the stream crossing for more wrestling with the park's terrain.

C Loop
Distance: 3 miles
Trail: Narrow single track
Direction: Clockwise

This loop begins at the halfway point on the B Loop and is more of a on-duty biking experienced on the other loops. From the B Loop turn left onto the short two-way spur that crosses the equestrian trail. Similar to A and B loops, C Loop features a long series of switchbacks descending into a swamp at **Mile 2**. The trail bottoms out at a 180-degree turn and then begins the longest climb; a quarter of a mile ride up. Near **Mile 3** you reach the two-way spur and follow it to cross the equestrian trail and return to the B Loop.

D Loop
Distance: 4 miles
Trail: Narrow single track
Direction: Clockwise

This loop puts bikers along a ridge for a technical ride that includes slippery, off-camber segments of single track and short but steep climbs. Balance is everything on this loop and riders can expect far more scrapes than from the rest of the system.

D Loop extends off the A Loop a quarter mile after you pass the junction with the B Loop. Turn left onto the short two-way spur that crosses the equestrian trail. Stay left where when the loop splits into single track. Near **Mile 4** the single track rejoins the two-way spur to return to A Loop.

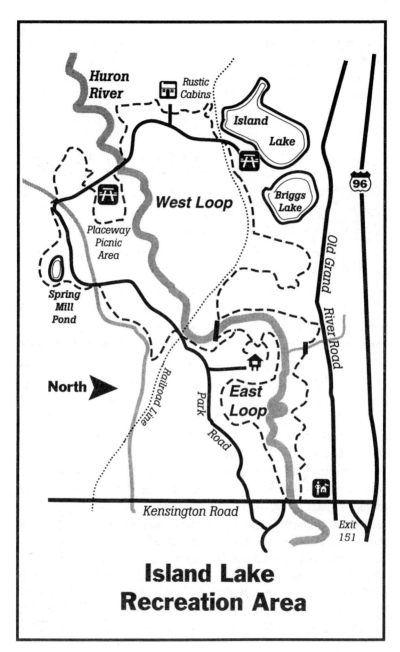

**Island Lake
Recreation Area**

Island Lake
Recreation Area

County: Livingston
Total Mileage: 13 miles
Terrain: Wooded hills, banks of the Huron River, open fields
Fees: Annual state park sticker or daily vehicle entry permit
Difficuty: Easy to moderate

Recent trail upgrades and re-routing by volunteers from the Michigan Mountain Biking Association has turned Island Lake Recreation Area into one of the most popular riding areas in southeast Michigan. Originally laid out for hiking, the trails now form a clearly marked 13-mile system that is both scenic and fun to ride.

Island Lake is a state park unit featuring forested hills, open fields, marshes and four lakes. The park's dominant feature, however, is the Huron River which winds for 7 miles through the middle of this 3,466-acre park. Popular with canoers during the summer, the Huron is also responsible for the more interesting stretches of the trail system which has made the park so popular with mountain bikers.

The staging for mountain bikers is at the Trailhead Parking Area, where access to the East and West loops is through a couple of short

two-way trails. Amenities include a parking area, vault toilets, picnic tables and drinking water. The Island Lake trail system has two large display maps, one at the park headquarters and the other at the Trailhead Parking Area.

The East Loop requires more skill than the West Loop and is best suited for intermediate and advanced riders. Almost entirely in the woods, the trail follows one bank of the Huron River and then returns along the opposite side. The West Loop is better suited for beginners and has more open fields and a convenient place to stop along the Huron River. When combined, the two loops provide a good 13-mile workout.

Getting There: From I-96, depart at exit 151 just east of Brighton. Head south on Kensington Road, pass the park headquarters on the corner of Grand River Road and cross the Huron River. The park entrance is on the east side of Kensington Road and at a contact station here you can purchase a motor vehicle entry permit and obtain a map. Trailhead Parking Area is reached by following the park drive to the right.

Information: Contact the park at Island Lake Recreation Area, 12950 East Grand River, Brighton, MI 48116; ☎ (313) 229-7067.

East Loop

Distance: 5 miles
Trail: Single Track
Direction: Clockwise

This route begins at the west end of the parking lot as either a two-track or a very twisty piece of single track. These spurs lead to the established trail, where you turn left and follow a fast two-way track through a stand of pines. The trail then drops down a steep gravel hill (*be alert for oncoming hikers!*) and rockets the rider up to the Riverbend Parking Area.

Before reaching it, turn right for a short jog through the woods

Mountain bikers with two tandems pause along the trail at Island Lake Recreation Area.

and over the Huron River to a junction with the West Loop. Follow the right fork as the East Loop, now a single track trail, begins climbing.

The first two miles are a hilly, rollicking roller coaster ride through the woods with some potential for speeds in the 20 mph range. At **Mile 1.5** the trail heads left and steeply descends a ravine to cross Mann Creek along a narrow bridge. It's a rough climb out with an off-camber right turn at the top.

On top of the ridge, the trail passes through a bit of woods and then moves into fields before challenging you with a downhill stretch that includes a fast right turn along the backside. From here to Kensington Road, the halfway point, the trail is a delightful, twisty, fast ride, mostly through open fields.

At **Mile 2.7**, the trail uses the Kensington Road Bridge to cross the Huron River. Turn right at the road, ride with traffic across the bridge and look for the trail post on the right. The next stretch is an open field ride loaded with S-turns before the trail climbs into the woods along the Huron River. On a hot summer afternoon, this shady section is especially pleasant.

After several big climbs, you emerge at a junction at **Mile 4.8**. The two-track to the left heads to the Trailhead Parking Area.

West Loop

Distance: 8 miles
Trail: Single Track
Direction: Clockwise

This loop has been increased from the original 7 miles with several rerouting and bypasses and now totals 8 miles. All the better. The West Loop begins at the Trailhead Parking Area with the same pair of two-way trails as the East Loop. After intersecting the main trail turn left and follow this two-way track through a stand of pines. The trail then drops down a steep gravel hill and climbs towards the Riverbend Parking Area.

It crosses the driveway for Riverbend and rolls into the woods to parallel the park road a bit. After popping onto the road, you pass underneath the Chesapeake and Ohio Railroad bridge. Once through, look to the left for the trail sign at the gate.

Here the trail runs along the tracks and includes some whoop-dee-doo hills. These are a series of small hills that get you warmed up before the trail heads into the woods. Just out of the woods you ride down a short, but steep, hill and then head into a series of S-curves in an area of semi-open fields and woods.

At **Mile 1.8**, the trail turns left just before the park road and then parallels it. You cross a wet area and then head to Spring Mill Pond. This is a popular fishing spot, stocked every spring with rainbow trout.

After turning left, away from the road, the trail whirls through thee woods for a spell and then climbs a hill. After reaching the tops, the trail moves through some secondary growth and then offers a good downhill run followed by a double-decker uphill at **Mile 2.6**.

You roll through more woods and fields before popping out at the parking area for the Placeway Picnic Area near **Mile 4**. The area has picnic tables, vault toilets and a cool river to dip the toes into. From the corner of the parking lot, the trail heads to the right and onto the roadway to cross the Huron River. After the bridge, watch for the trail marker on the left that leads you up a hill of mature trees.

After a loose section, the trail spins along the woods and into the fields where the park's rustic cabins are located. At **Mile 5** you cross the park road, then the railroad tracks and finally turn right to parallel the tracks along a wide two-track. The trail takes a brief turn into the woods where there is a surprise downhill and a loose uphill then resumes paralleling the tracks.

At **Mile 6.3** the trail turns away from the fields for a hilly stretch in the woods that offers some fun technical practice. It moves into the fields again, turns left and briefly parallels the railroad once more before descending to meet the outbound East Loop at **Mile 7.8**.

After passing the East Loop on the left, you cross a cement bridge over the Huron River. You finish this loop the same way as riders do on the East Loop with a connector spur leading to a steep, gravel climb and then a run through the woods. Turn right at the marker for Trailhead Parking Area to return to your car and finish the 8-mile ride.

Brighton Recreation Area features the hilly forested terrain and reclaimed farmlands that makes mountain biking so delightful in Livingston County and northern Washtenaw County.

Brighton
Recreation Area

County: Livingston
Total Mileage: 7 miles
Terrain: Rolling forested hills and open fields
Fees: Annual state park pass or daily vehicle entry permit
Difficulty: Easy to moderate

The moraines and other glacial features of Brighton Recreation Area gives the state park unit a trail system that is hilly and fun. Like many Southeast Michigan parks, the terrain at Brighton is primarily second growth forests and reclaimed farmlands. But the most dominant features here are the hills and riders will encounter them in all sizes and degree of inclines. The trail bed itself alternates from hard-pack to some patches of soft sand.

The two trails at Brighton are short and often favored by beginners, who quickly discover that it helps to know some climbing techniques. Two of the descents generate enough speed that first time riders should seek out the advice of experienced bikers on how to safely navigate the roots. Overall, however, these trails were originally designed for hiking so you won't find narrow S-turns that demand tight handlebar navigating.

There are modern restrooms and drinking

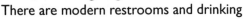

water at the parking area while the day-use area at Bishop Lake includes a beach, picnic tables, shelter and more restrooms.

Getting There: From I-96, just west of US-23, depart at exit 145 and head south on Grand River Avenue into Brighton. Once in the downtown area, head west on Brighton Road for 3 miles and then south on Chilson Road. At the park headquarters on Chilson Road, turn east on Bishop Lake Road and follow it 1.5 miles to the day-use area on Bishop Lake. The trailhead is near the end of the parking lot.

Information: Contact Brighton Recreation Area, 6360 Chilson Rd, Rt. 3, Howell, MI 48843; ☎ (810) 229-6566.

Kahchin Trail

Distance: 1.5 miles
Trail: Single Track
Direction: Clockwise

Both loops use the same trailhead and share the first half mile. You begin with a small but steep hill and then follow the outgoing left-hand fork to cross a dirt road. The descent into the woods on the other side features some subtle, nontechnical turns.

You meander in and out of the woods and then climb to cross a snowmobile trail that will be overgrown in the off-season. The ride is level here on a hard-pack track that alternates between grassy meadows and dappled shade.

The first significant climb and descent is reached before the junction between the Kahchin and Penosha trails and has roots, rocks, and signs of erosion that result in a little lumpy-bumpy action. It should be handled with some alertness, especially by novices. At the end of the hill you turn left onto a softer trail that takes you through open fields and then to the trail junction.

Kahchin heads south (right) as a level trail that can be spectacular in late spring when it is filled with dogwood in bloom. During the summer you'll often find yourself racing mosquitos

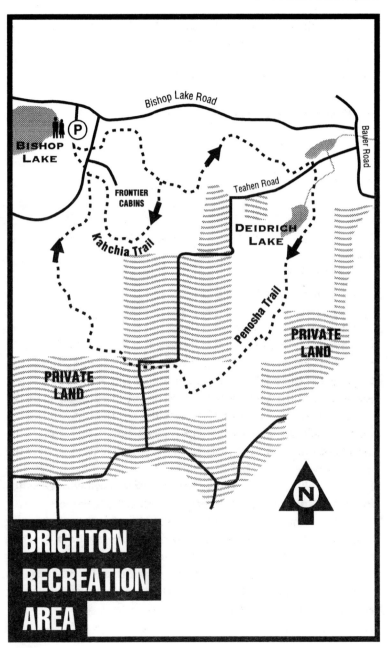

Bishop Lake Road

Bauer Road

BISHOP LAKE

P

FRONTIER CABINS

Teahen Road

Kahchia Trail

DEIDRICH LAKE

Penosha Trail

PRIVATE LAND

PRIVATE LAND

N

BRIGHTON RECREATION AREA

and deer flies. The wooded scenery is replaced by open fields as the trail climbs a small rise near the end. At this point Kahchin rejoins the Penosha Trail and crosses the dirt road, to the trailhead and parking lot.

Penosha Trail

Distance: 5 miles
Trail: Single track
Direction: Clockwise

The two trails share the first half mile as described above. At the junction, the Penosha heads east at the fork and at **Mile 1** reaches a tough climb with lots of roots, sand and opportunities for aerobic exercise. Here the scenery is wooded with some old growth trees and an understory that includes dogwood and some wildflowers.

At **Mile 1.5** the trail crosses Teahen Road and resumes on the opposite side and moves along Deidrich Lake. For the most part you're in thick woods where there are several sections of rough trail before a monster climb at **Mile 2.5**.

The track up the hill is soft, loose, sort of like peanut butter, and turns at the top. Try to climb it or save some energy and walk up. Watch for changes in this hill in the future as it could use a re-route.

At **Mile 3** there is a steep, sandy ascent that leads you to Teahen Road. Head west (left) onto Teahen Road and follow it 0.4 mile to where the road turns sharply south at a highway sign. The Penosha Trail is picked up again just right of this sign where a fence forms a border between the park and residential property.

Maintenance along the trail includes erosion bars to prevent water from flowing full speed down the hills. Quite a few are reached just before **Mile 4.5**. They are made with recycled conveyor belt material and are flexible but are still a challenge to climb over. From the water bars it's all downhill to the parking lot and dayuse area at Bishop Lake.

Pinckney Recreation Area

County: Washtenaw and Livingston
Total Mileage: 24.6 miles
Terrain: Hilly and rolling woods
Fees: Daily vehicle entry permit or annual state park pass
Difficulty: Moderate to strenuous

Pinckney State Recreation Area is a generous state park offering 10,842 acres of lakes and woods and many opportunities to camp, fish, boat, swim and hike. Today this park on the Washtenaw and Livingston county border is something of a Mecca for mountain bikers. More than 115,000 riders use the trail system annually, making Pinckney the most popular biking destination in Michigan.

The park contains three, single track trails that all begin from a common trailhead. Silver Lake, Crooked Lake and Potawatomi trails make up a 24.6-mile system that skirts the shoreline of many ponds, marshes and seven major lakes, including Crooked, Halfmoon, Gosling, Hiland and Blind lakes.

Collectively, the trails are referred to as the Potawatomi Trail System, the Poto or simply as the 'Pot' by many locals. Due to its popularity among cyclists, the park was forced to build a separate "Hiker's Only" trail in 1996 and mountain bikers themselves are urged to avoid the system during peak weekend times in the summer.

With the exception of the Silver Lake loop, the trail system is generally regarded as a challenging for advanced bikers, involving numerous hills and ridges to negotiate. The biggest problem with bikers in the park said one staff member is "too many beginners riding the Potawatomi that shouldn't be on it, resulting in a number of accidents."

The Silver Lake dayuse area serves as the trailhead for all three routes and features a beach and bathhouse, vault toilets, water and picnic area. Just before entering the dayuse area you pass the park headquarters where there is an ouside display with trail maps.

Getting There: From I-94, east of Jackson, depart at exit 159 and head north on M-52 to North Territorial Road. Turn east on North Territorial Road and in 6 miles head north on Dexter Townhall Road to reach the Silver Lake area in a mile. The trailhead is south of the lower parking lot. North Territorial Road can also be reached from US-23 at exit 49, 6 miles north of Ann Arbor.

Information: Contact Pinckney Recreation Area, 8555 Silver Hill Road, Pinckney, MI 48169, ☎ (313) 426-4913. For current trail conditions the Potawatomi Chapter of the Michigan Mountain Biking Association at ☎ (313) 663-9940.

Silver Lake Loop

Distance: 2 miles
Trail: Single track
Direction: Clockwise

From the trailhead the trail climbs into the woods up a series of water bars to the service road, crosses the road and climbs again up a mixture of water bars and roots. You glide on rolling descents through some pines, then arrive at a junction at *Mile*

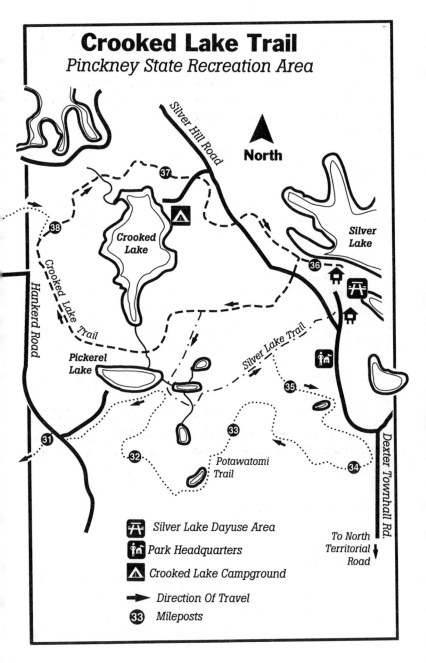

Crooked Lake Trail
Pinckney State Recreation Area

Silver Hill Road

North

37

38

Crooked Lake

Crooked Lake Trail

Hankerd Road

Silver Lake

36

Silver Lake Trail

Pickerel Lake

35

31

33

32

Potawatomi Trail

34

Dexter Townhall Rd.

To North Territorial Road

Silver Lake Dayuse Area

Park Headquarters

Crooked Lake Campground

Direction Of Travel

33 Mileposts

0.5 where the Potawatomi Trail is the left-hand fork heading south.

Stay right to continue the Silver Lake Loop along a series of hills and past a stone fireplace at ***Mile 0.7***. The fireplace is what remains of an early Irish family homestead. The next half mile is a mixture of roots, rocks and hills that leads to a second junction with the Potawatomi Trail.

Stay right again to ride between Pickerel Lake and a smaller lake to the east along a bridge that provides a panoramic view. Near ***Mile 1.5*** the Silver Lake route intersects with the Crooked Lake Trail coming in from the west (left). After a few more hills, you turn right at Silver Hill Road and in a few hundred yards turn left down the water bars to the trailhead.

Crooked Lake Trail

Distance: 5 miles
Trail: Single track
Direction: Clockwise

This hilly trail also winds through beautiful woods, and has the usual assortment of rocks and roots. The first leg of it is the Silver Lake Trail described above. At ***Mile 1.4*** you turn west (left) at the junction and cross a bridge over a short river that flows from Crooked Lake into Pickerel Lake, another scenic spot in the park.

Near ***Mile 2.5*** the trail enters a stand of wind-damaged oaks and then passes an access spur to Hankerd Road. You will roll through the forest to ***Mile 3*** where the return Potawatomi loop rejoins from the west (left). After the two trails merge into one, you descend into a ravine, cross another bridge and begin the longest climb of the loop.

This hill pretends to crest but then turns left and climbs some more for almost a half mile. There is a brief downhill between the first and second half with the top finally in sight at ***Mile 3.6***. A bench has been placed at this 1,008-foot highpoint, where bikers can enjoy the view of Crooked Lake or simply catch their breath.

On the back side you can coast downhill for some recovery

The bridge between Watson and Halfmoon Lakes along the Potawatomi Trail in Pinckney Recreation Area.

time. The trail then crosses a spur from Silver Hill Road at **Mile 3.8** and another just beyond **Mile 4**. After looping through the woods the trail arrives at a "T" intersection. Turn right here.

You pop out onto Silver Hill Road near **Mile 4.7** where you turn left and follow the road for almost a half mile back to the post marking the short, water bar descent to the trailhead.

Potawatomi Trail

Distance: 17.5 miles
Trail: Single track
Direction: Clockwise

Potawatomi begins on the same half mile stretch of trail from the trailhead as the Silver Lake and Crooked Lake loops. It then splits south (left) and rolls through the trees. At **Mile 1** the trail pops out onto pavement at a small parking area returning to single-track at the Potawatomi sign marker.

Moderate climbs through rolling terrain lead you to **Mile 2.2** where there is a picnic table followed by a junction with a ski trail on the right. Head left.

Near **Mile 2.7** is a bypass that takes you left and around a wet area. Another wet area is reached at **Mile 3** and is circumvented by a new bridge. At this point the trail heads north towards the south end of Pickerel Lake until it reaches a junction with the Silver Lake Trail at **Mile 4**.

The Potawatomi swings to the west (left) here and briefly skirts the bluff above the lake before a descent and an abrupt right turn onto a two-track. Turn left onto the access road and head toward Hankerd Road, reached at **Mile 4.6**. Use caution at this busy road because it is at the bottom of a hill. Cross the road, turn right and look for the trail marker.

At **Mile 5** you are approaching the first of the famous Potawatomi climbs that test your technical climbing and wind. On top, you wind through the woods for a mile and then must aim for a footbridge at the bottom of a ravine. There is another descent at **Mile 6.4** that is challenging due to potholes in the trail. This is followed by the last in this cluster of tough climbs.

At the top of this climb is an intersection with the Waterloo\Pinckney Trail from the west. The 35-mile backpacking trail stretches across Waterloo and Pinckney state recreation areas but is closed to bikers west of this junction. The Potawatomi heads straight and descends on a scattering of water bars to **Mile 7**, where it crosses the access road to Blind Lake. This spot on Blind Lake serves as a walk-in camping area for backpackers and features a pair of vault toilets.

Across the access road, you make a long climb to where the trail plateaus with a half mile gift of smooth rolling fun. But the ride gets technical at **Mile 7.5** where a sign warns of a steep downhill. Bumping down the water bars on this descent and rolling through the trees takes you to **Mile 7.8** and a bridge over the river running between Halfmoon and Watson Lake. Walk the bikes across this bridge so you can pause for the excellent view of

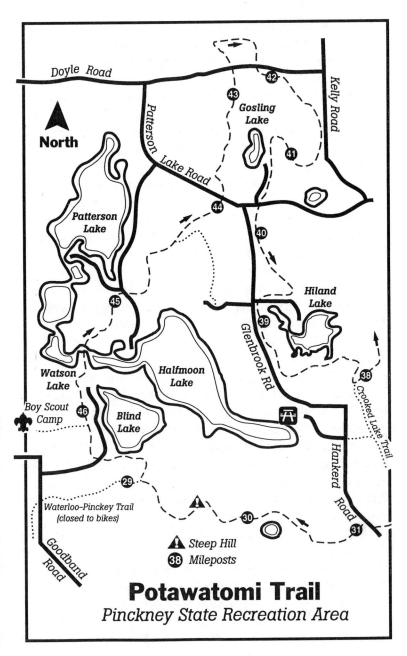

Potawatomi Trail
Pinckney State Recreation Area

the lakes and then ride to **Mile 8.3**, where you cross the access road to Patterson Lake.

At **Mile 8.8** there is an intersection with the extension loop. Turning north (left) on this loop adds 3.5 miles although this stretch can be very buggy during the summer because of the surrounding marshes. The extension crosses both Paterson Lake Road and Doyle Road and then skirts the tall fence marking U of M property before heading south. You finish on the dirt access road to Gosling Lake before re-crossing Patterson Lake Road.

Turning east (right) keeps the distance around 14 miles and puts you on a two-track at **Mile 9.4**. Follow it for a third of a mile until it crosses Glenbrook Road. After crossing the road, make a left and follow the two-track to the east (right). Turn south (right again) and you will be back on single track.

The junction with the extension loop is just before **Mile 10** where the trail swings to the right. This is followed by a scenic ride across the first of a series of footbridges finishing at **Mile 11**. You breeze through the next third of a mile to the junction with the Crooked Lake Trail. Head to the east (left).

Once on the Crooked Lake loop you will descend into a ravine, over a bridge, and begin the longest climb of the entire loop. This hill climbs for almost a half mile in two steps before rising to 1,008 feet at **Mile 12.3**.

You can coast downhill on the backside before crossing a spur from Silver Hill Road at **Mile 12.5** and again at **Mile 12.8**. Turn right at the "T" intersection and Silver Hill Road will be reached near **Mile 13.3**. Head south (right) for a half-mile ride back to the post that marks the short descent down water bars to the trailhead.

Maybury State Park

County: Wayne
Total Mileage: 3.5 miles
Terrain: Woods, fields, some hills
Fees: Daily vehicle entry permit or annual state park pass
Difficulty: Easy to moderate

This is a remarkable mountain biking trail and one of the few in Wayne County. It occupies a quarter of Maybury State Park, a 944-acre unit that at one time was a sanitarium. Today Maybury is a fully developed park that includes picnic areas, a working farm, bike and ski rentals, a horse stable and paved bikes paths as well as mountain biking trails.

The mountain biking trail was designed and built in 1994 as a winding system that makes the most of the rolling hills and dense woods found in the center of the park. The course is interesting but not fast and can be enjoyed in late fall as hunting is not allowed.

The 3.5-mile loop is mostly straightaways in the front half and then becomes technically difficult in the final third as you wrestle around trees and switch backs at off-camber angles. Beginners with a few rides under their belt and intermediate bikers should easily be able to

81

handle this trail without too many spills.

The park hosts mountain biking festivals in the summer with events ranging from the Huffy Toss and Family Fun Rides to Mountain Bike Polo. Trails are closed to bikes from Dec. 16 through April 14 to accommodate the ski season. Call the park to check on conditions.

Most of the park amenities, including the living farm and bike/ski rentals, are clustered around the northwest corner of the park and reached from the park entrance on Eight Mile Road. The mountain bike trailhead is accessed through the horseman's entrance off of Beck Road. Facilities here include a seasonal pump and vault toilets.

Getting There: From I-96, depart at exit 159 and then head south on Beck Road. After crossing Eight Mile Road in 4 miles look for the horseman's entrance of the park on the west side of Beck Road. Turn right here to immediately pass the park headquarters and then follow the road to the staging area for horsemen and mountain bikers.

The trailhead for the mountain bike trail is actually 0.4 mile from the staging area along a two-track trail that can be ridden. That adds almost another mile to the ride and is not included in the mileage of the following description.

Information: Contact Maybury State Park, 20145 Beck Road, Northville MI 48167; ☎ (810) 349-8390.

Outside Loop
Distance: 3.5 Miles
Trail: Tight single track
Direction: Clockwise

Southeast of the parking lot is a two-track. Follow this trail past a gate and around the fishing pond almost half mile to the posted trailhead on your left.

The track enters the woods and immediately passes the re-

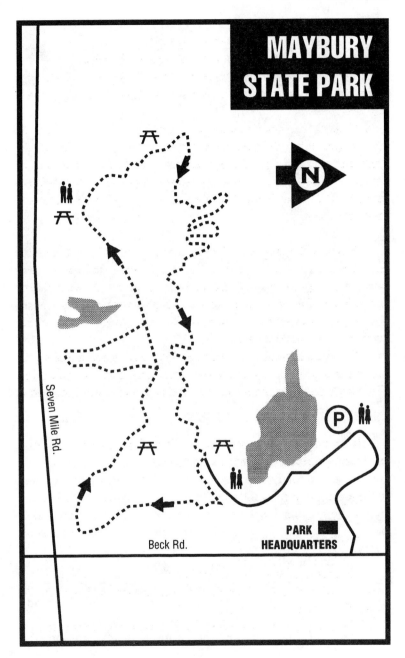

MAYBURY
STATE PARK

Mountain bikers take on a technical segment of the Maybury State Park trail system.

turn loop and then reaches junction at a bench. Head right before the bench and follow the single track as it slips through the trees for a quarter of a mile and then crosses a hiking trail. At **Mile 0.4** (from the trailhead, not the staging area), the track crosses a paved bike trail, where there is a rain shelter, and begins a slow climb.

The next half mile is a spin in and out of trees and brush, bypassing a wet section and finally reaching a junction with an extension spur. This spur adds another third of a mile to the ride and accesses terrain that is more interesting to ride.

At **Mile 1.7** is a junction; the main trail heads right into the woods while to the left is a short spur to the paved bike path. Turn right. This is where the fun begins, with the technical half of the loop. It was designed to be fun and also to keep speeds low in an effort to reduce erosion of the trail.

There's a lot more upper body work on this half, especially at **Mile 2,** where there is a nasty off-camber climb to the right. Even during dry conditions this climb is slippery but really gets your attention after a recent rainfall.

At **Mile 2.5** you're threading on switchbacks through beautiful woods and squeezing between giant trees. Finally, the trail loops around the edge of a bowl near the paved bike path and meets a two-track spur just beyond **Mile 3.** This connector allows bikers to bypass the final half mile back to the trailhead for additional loops on the trail system.

This final half mile back to the trailhead is interesting thanks to some fun cornering on climbs. At **Mile 3.3** you cross the paved bike path once more and then ride into some fragrant pines, rolling into the trailhead at **Mile 3.5.**

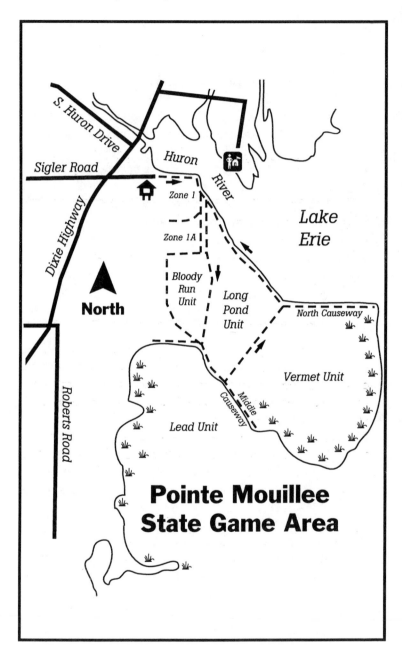

S. Huron Drive

Sigler Road

Dixie Highway

Huron River

Zone 1

Zone 1A

Bloody Run Unit

Long Pond Unit

Lake Erie

North Causeway

North

Roberts Road

Vermet Unit

Middle Causeway

Lead Unit

Pointe Mouillee State Game Area

Pointe Mouillee

Counties: Wayne and Monroe
Total Mileage: 7 miles
Terrain: Diked marshlands and ponds
Fees: None
Difficulty: Easy

Driving south along Jefferson Road in the "Downriver" region of Southeast Michigan, you pass a Detroit Edison plant with its towering twin smoke stacks. Then the Monsanto chemical company and finally the mammoth, pitch-black mill of McLoud Steel. One industrial complex after another.

It's hard to believe but one of the best birding areas in the state is just around the corner. That's what makes Pointe Mouillee State Game Area so unique. Within minutes in the rustbelt that is Downriver you go from a steel mill to one of the most extensive marshes in Michigan.

The state game area is 3,600 acres of marshes, pools and diked ponds surrounding the mouth of the Huron River and the shoreline of Lake Erie. Historically the marsh was much larger, so large that it's abundance of wildlife and waterfowl induced Late Woodland Indians to settle the area and then attracted French fur

traders in the 1700s who gave the marsh its name meaning "wet point."

In 1875, eight millionaire sportsmen purchased the area and formed the Big 8 Shooting Club, which four years later became the Point Mouillee Shooting Club, one of the oldest in the state. Eventually the fluctuating water levels of Lake Erie eroded the protective barrier island and the wetlands began to diminish, setting the stage in the early 1980s for one of the largest freshwater marsh restoration projects in the country.

Today the state game area is best known for its birding and waterfowl hunting. But bikers, in particular families and beginners, can also enjoy the area. From the end of Sigler Road, there are more than 7 miles of dikes, surrounding pools or flooded fields and topped by either a gravel work road or at least a well-beaten path.

The loop described is easy with no elevation gain and offers the opportunity to sight large numbers of ducks, herons and egrets as well as other wildlife throughout much of the year.

Getting There: From I-75, depart at exit 27 and turn east on North Huron River Road for two miles. Turn south on Jefferson Road and in 1.5 miles turn east on Campau Road to reach the headquarters. Continue south and Jefferson turns into Dixie Highway and crosses the Huron River. Turn right on Sigler Road and drive to its end to reach a parking area and locked gate.

Information: Contact Pointe Mouillee State Game Area, 37205 Mouillee Rd., Rockwood, MI 48713; ☎ (313) 379-9692.

Point Mouillee State Game Area

Distance: 6 miles
Trail: Two-tracks and dikes
Direction: None

Sigler Road, east of Dixie Highway, is a dirt work road into the state game area. Within a third of a mile it ends at a designated parking area and locked gate. Park here and start your ride on the road beyond the gate. Within a half mile the road curves south and ends at a grassy dike, posted "Zone 1."

Continue along this dike which skirts a pond on one side and a partially flooded field of the other. In either one you could view a variety of birds or ducks exploding from the vegetation. Stay on the dike that heads south and avoid the short one that deadends in the middle of Zone 1.

Just before **Mile 1**, the dikes ends at a "1A" sign and a path takes over to continue south along Long Pond Unit. This pond is particularly scenic as it is fringed by cattails and has open water in the middle with a handful of muskrat lodges. Just beyond the pond you can view Lake Erie. At **Mile 1.8**, you reach Middle Causeway, a dike that extends a half mile along side the southern border of the Vermet Unit. To the right of you is the open water of the Lead Unit.

Backtracking to the dike around Long Pond Unit, you now head northeast (right) and at **Mile 3.5**, reach North Causeway. This dike extends more than half mile towards the open water of Lake Erie, quickly passing a pullover site, where duck hunters pull their boats over the causeway during the waterfowl season.

Backtrack again to the dike around Long Pond Unit, which now heads northwest (right). You pass another pullover site and at **Mile 5.5** arrive a pump station used to control water levels in the marshes and ponds. Backtrack the first half mile of the ride to return the parking area.

Saginaw Bay

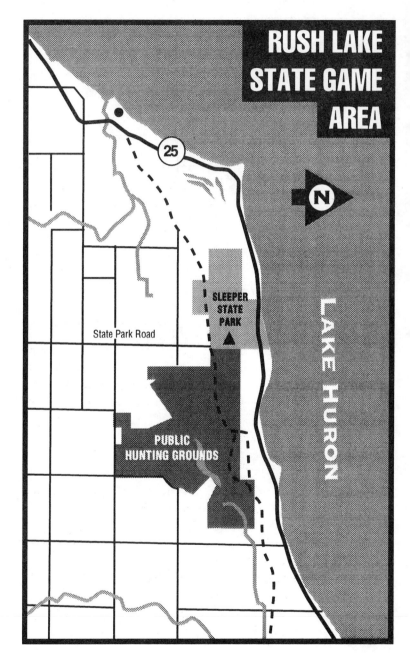

RUSH LAKE STATE GAME AREA

N

25

SLEEPER STATE PARK

State Park Road

PUBLIC HUNTING GROUNDS

LAKE HURON

Sleeper State Park

County: Huron
Total Mileage: 4.5 miles
Terrain: Level forest
Fees: Annual state park pass or daily vehicle entry permit
Difficulty: Easy to moderate

Sleeper State Park is currently using a small portion of its 700 acres for trails. Initially a nature trail, the system is now open to bikes and provides a scenic tour in beech and maple forests on the edge of Saginaw Bay. The trails are also heavily used by hikers and campers during the busy summer tourist season; caution and good biking etiquette are strongly advised.

Two trailheads are south of the campground with the main one located near the Outdoor Center's council fire ring off of State Park Road. The other route to ride is Sand Road, located a half mile south of the Outdoor Center. This dirt road continues east into the Rush Lake State Game Area and offers added distance and and the opportunity to enjoy the beauty of the rolling plains that border Saginaw Bay.

Sleeper State Park also features a wide, sandy beach, and a 280-site campground with full hook-ups, restrooms and showers.

93

Getting There: From Bay City head east on M-25 to skirt the tip of the Thump. The park entrance is 5 miles northeast of Caseville with the beach north of the road and the campground on the south side. Just beyond the main entrance is State Park Road where you head south to reach the park's headquarters and the trailhead at the Outdoor Center.

Information: Contact Sleeper State Park, 6573 State Park Road, Caseville, MI, 48725; ☎ (517) 856-4411.

Deer Run and Ridges Nature Trail

Distance: 4.8 miles
Trail: Single track.
Direction: Clockwise.

From the Council Fire Ring ride north on the connector called the Beach Trail for a quarter mile to where it intersects the metaphorically named Mile Circle Trail. Turn left here and then left again at the next intersection which will put you on the Ridges Nature Trail. The first stretch is in the woods, a blend of rolling terrain in a mature forest. The trail soon skirts a marsh and then returns to its wooded setting.

The trail continues to wind until you return to the Mile Circle Trail at **Mile 1**. Make a right and then a left to end up on the Beach Trail for a return to the Outdoor Center.

After arriving at the Council Fire Ring, ride clockwise on the Deer Run Trail. This route features a gentle rolling pace and isn't techincal at all, making it an ideal ride for those new to mountain biking. There are a few mounds along this 2.5-mile loop but no hills and little sand. There's little underbrush or other entanglements but along the way you'll pass under several impressive old growth trees.

Still not tired? Continue south along Sand Road into Rush Lake State Game Area for additional mileage.

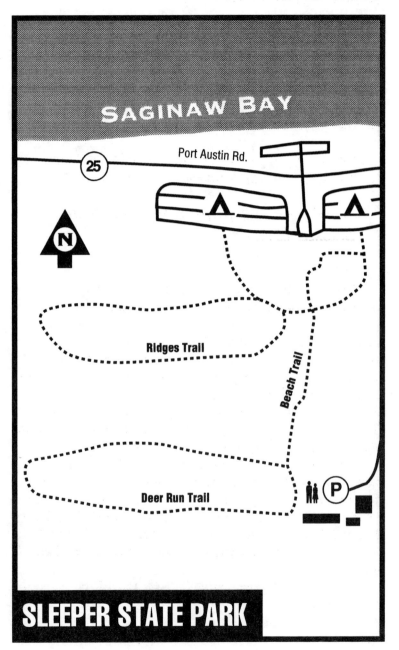

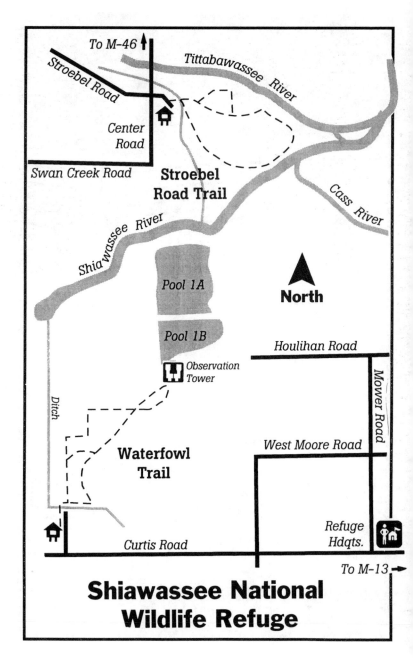

Shiawassee National Wildlife Refuge

Shiawassee National Wildlife Refuge

County: Saginaw
Total Mileage: 9 miles
Terrain: Wooded and flooded fields of a water-fowl preserve
Fees: None
Difficulty: Easy

Shiawassee National Wildlife Refuge, one of two federal refuges in Michigan, is a 8,984-acre preserve of marshes, pools, farm units and forests lying in one of the great confluences in the state. Four rivers - the Shiawassee, Flint, Cass and Tittabawassee - converge here making it a major rest area for waterfowl migrating north or south, especially Canada geese.

At times during the height of migration, more than 20,000 geese will gather on the refuge and even a greater number of ducks. You can often sight birds when driving the roads that border the refuge but the best place to see wildlife is along the Waterfowl Trail, which features an observation tower and a spotting scope.

This figure-eight loop is open to both hikers and mountain bikers and follows gravel dikes and wide, wooded paths for an easy ride to the

97

A Mountain biker heads to the observation tower on the Waterfowl Trail in the Shiawassee National Wildlife Refuge.

tower. The trail is open year-round but to see a portion of the flight bikers should hit the trail from March through April for the spring migration or September through October for the fall migration. Keep in mind that during the October goose hunting season the trail is closed until 1 p.m. It is also closed during portions of Michigan's three-month deer season.

Also part of the Shiawassee National Wildlife Refuge, on the north side of the Tittabawassee River, is the Stroebel Road Trail, a network that includes the mile-long Marsh Loop and four-mile Woods Loop. The Woods Loop in particular has become a favorite of local riders as it passes through a forested area bordered on one side by the Tittabawassee River and on the other by the Shiawassee River.

You don't see the huge influx of waterfowl from this trail but you might spot deer or at the very least see their tracks as well as ride past a beaver lodge in a pond. This narrow single track has a few small rises and dips but it is a fairly easy ride for beginners.

Getting There: From I-75, depart at exit 149 and head west on M-46 (Holland Road) to M-13. Head south on M-13 for six miles and then west on Curtis Road, where you'll first pass the refuge headquarters and then reach the trailhead within 4 miles at the end.

To reach the Stroebel Road Trail continue on M-46, cross Saginaw River and turn south on Center Road. Cross the Tittabawassee River and then look for the refuge trail sign on the east side of the road. The parking lot and trailhead are just off Center Road.

Information: Contact the Shiawassee National Wildlife Refuge, 6975 Mower Rd., Rt. 1, Saginaw, MI 48601; ☎ (517) 777-5930.

Waterfowl Trail

Distance: 5 miles
Trail: Gravel road and dikes
Direction: None

The trailhead is posted along Curtis Road but actually begins just to the north on a gravel road. Here you'll find vault toilets, benches, an information display and a trail heading north. You cross a gravel dike and continue north on another dike heading between a series of fields, some flooded, others planted with corn.

Within a half mile from the parking area you pass a cut-off spur that shortens the ride to 1.5 miles and at **Mile 1** begin zig-zagging east through the woods until you come to a four-way junction near Ferguson Bayou at **Mile 2**. The observation platform is just a half mile to the left.

The tower, reached at **Mile 2.5**, is not high but it doesn't need to be. It overlooks more farm units and large pools and from this vantage point you can often spot great blue herons, egrets, a variety of ducks and usually dozens of Canada geese, depending on the time of year. The scope on the tower is a great aid indentifying the various species.

A different route back to the trailhead begins with a half-mile stretch through a flooded wooded area bordering Ferguson Bayou. Look for the muskrat and beaver lodges here. At **Mile 3** you return to the four-way junction reached earlier in the ride. Take a left and follow gravel dikes for some fast riding in the remaining 2 miles to the parking lot.

Stroebel Road Trails

Distance: 7 miles
Trail: Single track
Direction: Clockwise

The Stroebel Road Trail system is literally on the edge of a city and Saginaw is lucky. If there was ever a perfect escape from its urban grasp, this is it; a point of land where two great rivers converge to form a moat against the advances of what some people call progress and others decay. On the north side of the point there's the Tittabawassee, on the south side the Shiawassee. In between the two is an area of woods, marshes, creeks and five miles of trails open to many users, including mountain bikers.

The trailhead and parking lot are at the east end of Stroebel Road where both the four-mile Woods Loop and the mile-long Marsh Loop begin on the same path posted with a hiker symbol. Within minutes you arrive at a long bridge across a pond, where there is usually evidence of beaver activity, including a lodge, as well as interpretive signs explaining the nesting boxes that have been erected for wood ducks.

Just beyond the pond the trail cuts through a meadow and passes a second interpretive display before entering the woods for your first glimpse of the Tittabawassee River through the trees. At *Mile 0.7* is a well posted junction where the two loops diverge. Follow the left-hand fork to continue on the Woods Loop.

This loop heads back towards the Tittabawassee River which you can see after the trail climbs onto a dike. The dike keeps you dry despite the lowlying flood plains on both sides. You pass a bench and then descend the dike as the trail swings south.

At *Mile 2* you break out at a powerline. The trail then re-enters the woods as a flat single track, winding through the trees and at one point crossing a bridge over a sluggish stream. You emerge from the woods at a low lying area that includes a pair of ponds and usually hundreds of deer tracks. The route remains remarkably dry, thanks to recent work by the refuge staff and local mountain bikers.

The trail moves into an open meadow, recrosses the powerline right-of-way and finishes in the woods as a narrow single track to the trailhead.

A mountain biker crosses a bridge into Muskrat Flats at Ringwood Forest, a 160-acre unit of the Saginaw County Parks and Recreation Commission that includes a stretch of the Bad River.

Ringwood Forest

County: Saginaw
Total Mileage: 3.5 miles
Terrain: Woods and the Bad River
Fees: None
Difficulty: Easy

Ringwood Forest is a 160-acre unit of the Saginaw County Parks and Recreation Commission with one of the oldest forest plantations in the state. Part of a great pine forest that once covered Saginaw Valley, the area was completely logged in 1862 by Eleazer J. Ring. In 1883, Ring's son established a spruce plantation and today that section of the park, called Spruce Alley, is a magnificent stand of trees.

Ringwood's trail system is a series of four loops that can be combined for a 3-mile ride in the woods. Although there are a couple short slopes, this is an extremely easy route and ideal for novice riders, including children new to mountain biking.

Avoid these trails in the spring because the South Branch of the Bad River bisects the park and the surrounding flood plains make for sloppy biking. The best time by far is in October when

the trails are dry, the bugs are gone and the fall colors stunning. Generally you can count on the hardwoods in this region of the state to reach their peak colors in the second or third week of October.

Facilities include a picnic area with tables, grills, vault toilets, a shelter and water.

Getting There: From St. Charles head south on M-52 for 2 miles and then west on Ring Road. Within 2 miles Ring road ends at the park entrance.

Information: Contact the Saginaw Parks and Recreation Commission, 111 S. Michigan Ave., Saginaw, MI 48602; ☎ (517) 790-5280.

Ringwood Forest

Distance: 3 miles
Trail: Single track and two-track
Direction: None

The best way to ride the trails from the parking lot is to head towards the South Branch of the Bad River and begin with the Witch Hazel Loop. Follow the park road towards the canoe landing but continued onto the trail system via a bridge into Muskrat Flats. The flats are the floodplains surrounding the South Branch and often can be muddy or buggy or both during the summer.

Within a half mile you cross a second bridge over the sluggish river itself and then come to a posted junction. Turn right to follow the Witch Hazel Loop in a counter clockwise direction. The loop is a mile-long, level ride through the woods. You quickly pass a junction with the Pine Hills Run, a short spur that splits the loop in half. At **Mile 1.4**, you return to the the flood plains and recross the South Branch to heads towards the canoe landing.

The second half of the recommended ride is the Walnut Ridge Trail/Lumberjack Loop and you pick it up as soon as you hit the paved park road. Look for a trail sign to the left before the en-

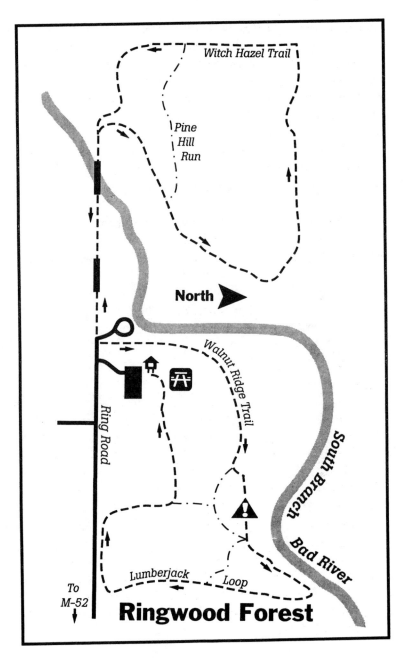

Witch Hazel Trail

Pine
Hill
Run

North ▶

Walnut Ridge Trail

Ring Road

South Branch

Bad River

Lumberjack   Loop

To
M-52

Ringwood Forest

trance to the dayuse area. Walnut Ridge Trail skirts the picnic area and passes a observation deck above the river and then a bench.

At **Mile 2**, you have a short downhill segment that is surprisingly steep for Saginaw County and then climb back up the river banks. Stay left at the junction that follows Post 1 and you take on two more short slopes. New riders or children should consider walking down the first one that immediately follows the junction because it takes some technical skill.

At **Mile 2.25** you pass Post 4 and a bench with a view of river's rippling waters below. Continue left at this intersection and in a few hundred yards you'll reach a second bench and view of the river at a spot known as Pike's Perch. From here the trail swings due south and you follow it back towards Ring Road. Where the trail loops north you enter Spruce Alley on a two-track and the pines tower above you on both sides.

At **Mile 2.8**, you arrive at a posted junction with the spur known as Pine Promenade. Turn left at the plaque dedicated to the Ring family and within a quarter mile you emerge in the dayuse area.

Pine Haven Recreation Area

County: Midland
Total Mileage: 10.2 miles
Terrain: Rolling and level woods
Fees: Donation
Difficulty: Easy

Pine Haven Recreation Area is a unit of the Midland County Parks and Recreation Commission and located just south of US-10. Originally laid out as a cross country system, the commission later opened up its wide and rolling trail system to off-road cycling. The pleasant wood setting and wide trails make this park ideal for beginners and intermediate riders.

Despite the limited size of the park, the numerous loops and intersections create a trail system with a variety of possibilities for riders. Much of the trail bed is clay amalgam but changes to loose sand on sections closer to the Salt River at the south end.

Because the trails were built for skiing, there are vault toilets but no water at the trailhead. Just 2 miles to the east is Sanford, where food and water can be obtained before or after the ride.

Getting There: The park is 6 miles northwest of Midland and practically borders US-10. Depart US-10 at West River Road and head south. Quickly turn west (right) onto Maynard Road which ends at the park entrance.

Information: Contact Midland County Parks and Recreation Commission, 1270 James Savage Road, Midland, MI 48640-5682; ☎ (517) 832-6870.

Outside Loop

Distance: 3.8 miles
Trail: Wide single track
Direction: Counter clockwise

From the west side of the parking lot, pick up the trail near the information display. The skating lane for skiers, a relatively flat trail, is to the right at the first intersection while straight ahead is the main trail for the Outside Loop. Stay right at the next intersection, Post A, again at Post B and for the rest of the trail to enjoy the longest possible ride on this system.

The trail stays relatively wide and rejoins the skating lane within a half mile from the start. Heading west now, you'll find the trail a casual ride through a rolling woods of mature trees. At **Mile 1** is Post C and at this intersection you head right for a descent from the high ground towards the river.

Just beyond Post C, you'll come to the first of many junctions with the Emergency Evacuation Road. Make a right here to parallel it briefly and then within a quarter mile follow the now sandy trail as it crosses the road. Near **Mile 1.5** is Post D and by heading right you loop towards the Salt River for a third of a mile before swinging up to Post E. At this intersection you turn right and head down into the flood plains along the river again.

The trail wanders back to the Salt River to a spot where there is a bench and a view on a bluff above the water. This makes a nice

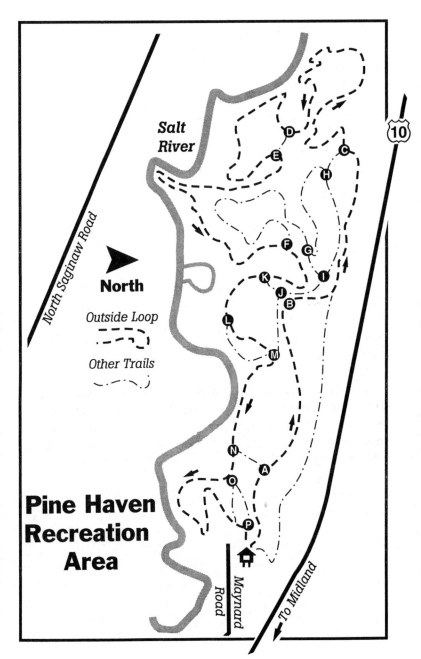

Salt River

North Saginaw Road

North

Outside Loop

Other Trails

Pine Haven Recreation Area

Maynard Road

To Midland

10

spot for a rest, especially in the fall when occasionally you can spot steelhead trout spawning upstream.

After briefly skirting the river, you ascend into the park's forest, where the trail passes through a quick series of intersections, beginning with Post F at *Mile 2.8*. Stay right at them all; Post F, Post G, Post K and finally Post L, where a right turn puts you on a spur that heads to the river before looping back to Post M at *Mile 3.3*.

You now have a maze of choices on how to return to the trailhead and parking lot. If you continue to stay right at each intersection, including Post O, you will enjoy one last spur down to the Salt River and a ride of 3.8 miles. A left onto either of the other two trails at Post O will send you directly back to the parking lot for a 3.6-mile workout.

Tobico Marsh

County: Bay
Total Mileage: 5 miles
Terrain: Woods, marshland
Fees: Daily vehicle entry fee or annual state park pass
Difficulty: Easy

Tobico Marsh is a 1,800-acre wildlife refuge that is part of the Bay City State Recreation Area and almost within sight of the city itself. The refuge features a pair of loop trails; one and four miles in length, and is connected to the rest of the state park unit by the Frank Andersen Rail-Trail.

The trails are open to mountain biking and can be combined for an easy, 6-mile round-trip from the park's Saginaw Bay Visitors Center. When enjoyed during the fall and spring bird migrations, this outing combines a ride through the woods with the opportunity to observe large numbers of ducks and geese from a pair of observations towers overlooking Tobico Marsh.

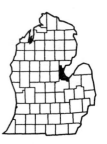

The refuge contains a variety of habitats, including small pockets of cattail marshes, oak/maple climax forest and Tobico Lagoon, a 900-acre body of water and the largest remaining wetland along Saginaw Bay. During the fall more than 4,000 ducks and geese gather in the marsh, with the number increasing to almost 10,000 during the peak migration from late October to early November.

Families should plan on first visiting the Saginaw Bay Visitors Center, the newest state park interpretive center in Michigan. The center features hands-on exhibits and displays that explain the history and wildlife of both Saginaw Bay and Tobico Marsh. This portion of Bay City State Recreation Area also has restrooms, water, picnic areas, shelters, a modern campground and a dayuse area with a beach.

Getting There: Bay City State Recreation Area is 5 miles north of Bay City. From I-75, depart at exit 168 and head east on Beaver Road which ends in 5 miles at the park entrance just past the intersection with M-247.

To reach the Tobico Marsh trailhead, head north (right) on M-247 for a half mile and then west on Killarney Road to the posted entrance.

Information: Contact Bay City State Recreation Area, 3582 State Park Dr., Bay City, MI 48706; ☎ (517) 684-3020.

Tobico Marsh Trail
Distance: 6 miles
Trail: Paved trail, wide single track
Direction: Counter clockwise

From the Saginaw Bay Visitors Center, you begin with the Andersen Nature Trail, a paved rail-trail to Tobico Marsh. To skip the rail-trail, begin the ride at the Tobico Marsh trailhead off of Killarney Beach Road.

Andersen Nature Trail heads north, first through a wooded tract and then into a large marshy area with pockets of open water. Along the way there are observation decks with benches, bike racks and interpretive plaques that describe the birds and wildlife you might encounter. Take a break from your ride, sit

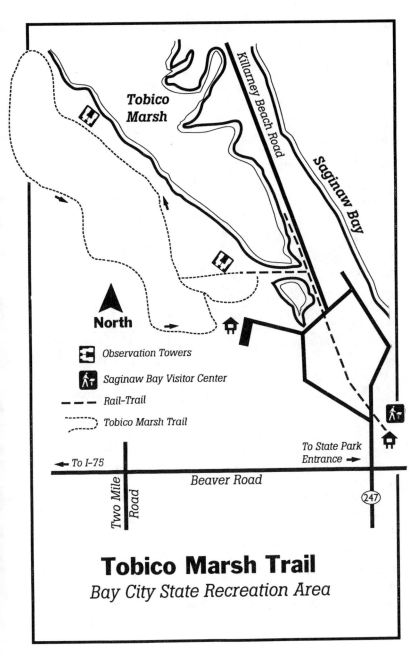

Tobico Marsh Trail
Bay City State Recreation Area

One of the highlights of mountain biking Tobico Marsh is the possibility of sighting a variety of waterfowl like these pintail ducks.

quietly in one of the observation decks and enjoy whatever flutters by.

Eventually the trail crosses Killarney Beach Road, returns to its marshy setting and arrives at a dike. Head west (left) on the dike to enter Tobico Marsh. Just before **Mile 1** the paved rail-trail ends at the first of two 30-foot observation towers. Continue due west on the path and then head north (right) onto the long loop at a junction marked by a display sign explaining maturing forests. The trail continues as a straight, wide path through a tunnel of towering trees. The foliage includes red and white oak, red maple and poplar, all of which are brilliant during October.

At **Mile 1.8**, the trail arrives at an interpretive area featuring the second observation tower, a boardwalk and vault toilets. The 300-foot boardwalk makes for an interesting break from riding as it extends beyond the thick growth of shoreline cattails into the open lagoon. Just as impressive is the sight from the top of the tower. It's a climb of 60 steps, but you can see a good portion of the lagoon, including a grassy islet in the middle that attracts waterfowl in spring and fall.

From the tower, the trail continues north and then swings south at **Mile 2.3**, quickly passing between two cattail marshes. In another half mile, you wind through a grove of paper birch and then move into an open forest. The trail crosses a bridge and then at **Mile 4.5** emerges at a parking area and second trailhead for Tobico Marsh. Facilities here include a shelter, benches and vault toilets.

From the shelter it's a short ride to the junction between the two loops. Head east (right) as the trail crosses three bridges, each spanning an old beachline left by the retreating Lake Huron centuries ago. At **Mile 5**, you return to the paved rail-trail and the first observation tower. Backtrack along Andersen Nature Trail to return to the Saginaw Bay Visitors Center.

Southwest Michigan

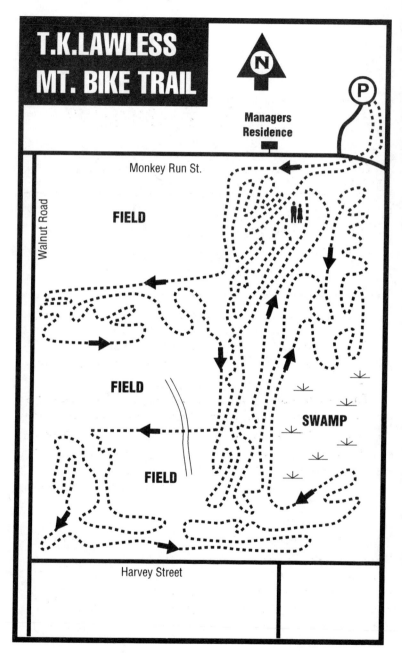

T.K. LAWLESS MT. BIKE TRAIL

N

Managers Residence

Monkey Run St.

Walnut Road

FIELD

FIELD

FIELD

SWAMP

Harvey Street

T. K. Lawless County Park

County: Cass
Total Mileage: 10.5 miles
Terrain: Forests, fields and hills
Fees: Vehicle entry fee
Difficulty: Easy

There's a saying handed down from those who inhabited Michigan long before the rest of us showed up: The truth requires very few words.

That captures the feeling of the system at T.K. Lawless County Park. This trail sums up what mountain biking is all about - the right feeling. There are trails all across the state, from routes as flat as a paper plate to those with enough vertical to get you started well on your way to the moon. Good trails, however, all have one thing in common and that's a feeling about how it is laid out and how it rides.

A well-designed trail will have that feeling regardless of where it is located. T.K. Lawless County Park, located in a rural setting in the heart of Cass County, is the classic example. At first glance this 640-acre park does not appear to be an ideal mountain biking site. But spend an afternoon here and you'll dis-

cover the trail is a fun ride through a surprisingly rolling terrain of woods, fields and swamps.

There are no long climbs along the system so beginners will find the ride fun and not overly tiring. On the other hand, when the trail is ridden at speed, intermediate and advanced riders will have their bike handling skills put to the test.

The system is well-signed with blue and yellow markers that, barring any vandalism, should last a long time. The trail itself follows every nuance and dip in the land and includes rocks, roots and logs as if Mother Nature had intended a mountain biking playground for us to enjoy.

Though many parts of the trail nearly intersect each other as they wind back and forth, in the summer the heavy foliage keeps each stretch of track hidden from the others. In the fall, views are much more open and you easily see how close the loops lie to each other.

The trail was designed by Steve Barns of the Michigan Mountain Biking Association and built by the Cass County Parks & Recreation Department and MMBA volunteers.

The riding season at Lawless County Park is spring through fall. Facilities include flush toilets, water and a picnic area. On the north side of Monkey Run Street is an interesting trail for hikers around Doane Lake.

Getting There: The county park is located just south of M-60 between Three Rivers and Cassopolis near Vandalia in Cass County. Two miles west of Jones, the park is posted on M-60 and is reached by turning south on Lewis Lake Road and then east on Monkey Run Street. The park is a mile up Monkey Run Street.

Information: Contact Cass County Parks and Recreation, 340 O'Keef St., Cassopolis, MI 49031; ☎ (616) 445-8611.

Lawless County Park Trail

Distance: 10.5 miles
Trail: Single track
Direction: Counter clockwise

From the parking lot the trail follows a small strip of woods and then crosses Monkey Run Street. On the south side of the road, the trail meanders through the woods in such a way that your eyes and legs become one in constant zigzag motion, like a river tumbling effortlessly down a hill. In the fall, you can see Walnut Road through the trees before you cross a two-track road cutting from one corn field to another at **Mile 2**.

At **Mile 3.6**, the trail parallels Harvey Road, which can be used for an early return to the parking lot. Follow the road west and then head north on Walnut Road to Monkey Run Street. The trail, on the other hand, begins to wind its way north, skirting a large swamp. The swamp is visible in the fall but not in the summer when the foliage is heavy on the trees.

You pass confidence markers and maps every mile or two along the system and at **Mile 6.2** arrive at a trail sign which marks a short cut back to the parking lot. The main route heads south from the trail sign.

A second shortcut to the parking lot is passed at **Mile 7.8**, while the main trail continues to the south. Just before **Mile 8**, you'll reach a rest area with vault toilets and a water pump. The trail then heads south once more, traversing back and forth through the woods for more than 2 miles before emerging at the rest area again at **Mile 10**. You cross Monkey Run Street one more time and quickly reach the parking lot within a half mile.

A cyclist enters an open field at the Al Sabo Land Preserve. A small portion of the 740-acre tract near Kalamazoo was opened recently to mountain biking.

Al Sabo Land Preserve

County: Kalamazoo
Total Mileage: 5.9 miles
Terrain: Woods, open fields, marshes
Fees: None
Difficulty: Easy to moderate

The Al Sabo Land Preserve is not a public park, but a working water well field that protects Atwater Mill Pond, the headwaters of Portage Creek and an important source of water for the City of Kalamazoo. The interesting topography of the area, which includes broadleaf forests, extensive wetlands and 80-foot high ridges bordering the mill pond and creek, has always attracted a variety of users.

But due to excessive erosion, the 750-acre preserve was closed in 1992 to all visitors by the Kalamazoo Public Services Department and not re-opened until 1994, when new rules and restrictions were drawn up. Working with a variety of environmental groups, the department has recently designated a 5.9-mile loop for mountain bikers within in its trail system.

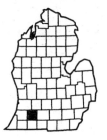

Although the mileage is not extensive, the

loop is a scenic and interesting ride. There are a few downhill stretches and climbs where the trail dips off the ridges into the Portage Creek drainage area, but overall the route is easy and within the ability of most novice riders. Its location, a mere 10-minute drive from I-94, makes it perfect for anybody needing to stretch their legs during that long haul across the state.

The vast majority of users at Al Sabo, however, are hikers and although the trail system attempts to keep them separated from bikers, you will inevitably encounter a few. It's important to avoid conflict by staying on the designated route and slowing down and walking your bike past hikers on narrow sections of trail. Conflict-generating behavior or excessive erosion and mountain bikers will again lose access to this area. In the winter, the park is popular with Nordic skiers.

Facilities at the trailhead are limited to a gravel parking area and a trailhead display area.

Getting There: From I-94, on the west side of Kalamazoo, depart at exit 72 and head south on 9th Street. In a half mile, 9th Street curves west into O Avenue and passes Kalamazoo Valley Community College. Continue south on 8th Avenue for Texas Corner but just before reaching the intersection turn left or north-east on Texas Drive. Within a mile you'll reach a posted parking lot for the Al Sabo Land Preserve.

Information: Contact the Kalamazoo City Parks Department at ☎ (616) 337-8191 or the Kalamazoo City Water Department at ☎ (616) 337-8002.

Al Sabo Land Preserve
Distance: 5.9 miles
Trail: Single track, two-track and gravel road
Direction: Counter clockwise
The trail departs from the north side of the parking lot and immediately comes to a junction where hikers continue north

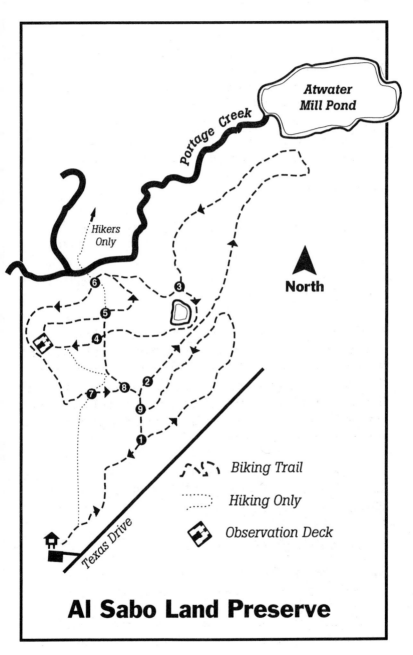

Atwater Mill Pond

Portage Creek

Hikers Only

North

🔲 Biking Trail

········· Hiking Only

🏠 Observation Deck

Texas Drive

Al Sabo Land Preserve

into an open field and mountain bikers curve east onto a wide, wooded path. Be alert as this first segment handles two-way traffic. Within a half of a mile you break out into a field and arrive at Post 1 at an intersection with a two-track. Continue in a northeast direction on the wide single track for a loop through an open field.

This segment is easy and, after passing through a small stand of pines, you arrive back at the two-track and Post 9 at *Mile 1.5*. Head right (north) on the two-track to quickly reach Post 2, where you head right again.

You continue along a two-track in a northeast direction, but within a mile the trail switches to a single track and at *Mile 2.5* arrives at the best downhill run of the system; steep for beginners, more than manageable for all others. At the bottom the trail curves southeast and becomes a winding route through the woods to Post 3 at *Mile 3.2*. Here you make a left to an easy climb and then skirt a marshy area, where occasionally there are some ducks on the small patch of open water in the middle.

Within a half mile you reach Post 4, an intersection back at the two-track, and shoot across it to continue west on a single track. Within a quarter mile the trail passes an observation platform and then returns east as a rough road, recrossing the two-track at Post 5 at *Mile 4.2*.

Stay on the road, which has a loose gravel surface as it descends quickly towards Portage Creek. It bottoms out at Post 6 and then swings west past a scenic marsh that the creek passes through. Just beyond the marsh the route returns to being a single track and climbs gently away from Portage Creek through a heavily wooded area.

Post 7 is reached at *Mile 5.2* and shortly after that is Post 8, located across from Post 2 on the two-track. Head south on the two-track to Post 1 and backtrack the first segment to return to the trailhead and parking lot for a ride of just under 6 miles.

Allegan
State Game Area

County: Allegan
Total Mileage: 21 miles
Terrain: Hardwood forests and flooded wild-life areas
Fees: None
Difficulty: Moderate

Allegan State Game Area is a 45,000-acre wildlife preserve created in 1946 by combining several tracts of public land. The terrain includes seven lakes, bogs, open meadows and pine and hardwood forests that cover the sandy plains of west-central Allegan County. The area was created as a wildlife refuge and during the fall migration 75,000 to 100,000 Canada geese stop to rest before continuing their flight south as well as many species of waterfowl.

Recreation in the state game area includes camping, hiking, cross country skiing, fishing, hunting and mountain biking on the 21-mile network of trails. The trail system is extensive and composed of many loops but was built for skiing and, at best, is only lightly posted. At times it can be a challenge to follow and so sandy in places to point of being treacherous.

127

The state game area attracts only a small number of mountain bikers and that is the real attraction of this perserve. If you're burned out on the crowds at Yankee Springs or Fort Custer Recreation Areas or simply want more of a where-am-I? adventure, Allegan State Game Area can be a fun and interesting place to ride. During October, when the fall colors have set in and hundreds of geese are flying overhead, it can even be stunning.

For the most part, this route is the outside loop of the trail system with the exception of segments from Post C to Post D to Post E at the north end. This stretch is poorly marked and from Post C to Post D is extremely sandy. While this has no effect on skiers in the winter, mountain bikers will find these segments almost impossible to ride at times, resulting in walking their bikes.

The mileage can be easily shortened in many ways. For a 7.5-mile day, simply return to the trailhead from Post J by following the trail that parallels 118th Avenue to Post H and then to the refuge headquarters. For a scenic 5-mile ride begin at the trailhead and follow Posts B-G-F-J-H.

Facilities include water and vault toilets at the refuge headquarters near the main trailhead as well as Pine Point Campground, a rustic facility that includes a swimming area on Swan Creek Pond. If you're riding the trails during June or July, bring bug repellent as the mosquitoes and deer flies can be thick at times.

Getting There: From US-131, south of Grand Rapids, depart at exit 55 and head west on M-222. Within 10 miles, the road merges with M-89 in the town of Allegan, which should be followed north to Monroe Road. Head west on Monroe Road, where there is a state game direction sign. The road curves around Lake Allegan for 7 miles and then merges into 118th Avenue and crosses the Swan Creek Dam. In another quarter mile on 118th Avenue is the refuge headquarters and directly across is 46th Street which heads north a short ways to the main trailhead.

Information: Contact Allegan State Game Area, 4590 118th Ave., Allegan, MI 49010; ☎ (616) 673-2430.

The 21-mile trail system at Allegan State Game includes open fields, wooded stretches and dikes past flooded ponds, which in the fall attract thousands of geese.

Allegan State Game Area

Distance: 10.6 miles
Trail: Single track and two-track
Direction: Clockwise

From the trailhead parking area, head west towards the vault toilet and into the woods where the trail eventually swings to the north. The single track remains wooded until you reach a clearing with a noticeable downhill stretch. The trail then climbs into a red pine plantation, jogs briefly on an old two-track and then resumes north. Just past **Mile 1** you cross 46th Street and reach Post B on the other side. An option at this intersection is to continue to Post G and then Post F, a 1.5-mile ride along a very well defined and easy to follow trail.

The outside route continues north from Post B towards Post C along a trail that parallels 46th Street, a loose gravel road. Within a half mile you cross another gravel road that heads east to Post F. On the other side of the gravel road the trail resumes paralleling 46th Street.

At **Mile 2.4**, you arrive at the four-way intersection between 122nd Avenue and 46th Street. The trail crosses the intersection and continues west along a stretch that is difficilt to follow at times. There is just enough blue blazes (paint marks) on the trees to lead you to the edge of a large open field at **Mile 2.7** where the trail swings north.

At first the trail is in the open field, but then swings just inside the bordering trees. Either stretch is rough riding due to the extremely sandy soil. Post C is reached at **Mile 3** and from there you can depart the field by heading east into a lightly forested area along a single track that can be hard to recognize at times.

Everything changes after you cross 46th Avenue at **Mile 3.3**. On the other side you resume on a two-track for another half mile to Post E, where you head south and skirt a bluff overlooking the wildlife refuge portion of the state game area. In the fall, when the leaves have begun to drop, the views are good along

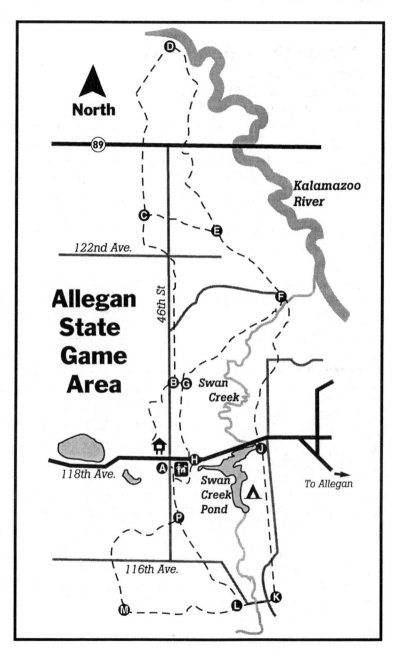

this stretch.

At **Mile 4.3**, the two-track comes to a gate and on the other side the trail returns to being a single track and swings away from the wildlife refuge. This section is fun; a long, but controlled, downhill run through the woods until you break out into a parking area. At the south end is Post F, reached at **Mile 4.8**. At this intersection you can take the crossover trail to Post G and eventually return to the trailhead.

The outside loop continues south towards Post J along a two-track, with a locked gate in the parking area. You quickly descend to a dam and skirt a wildlife marsh along a dike. The flooded marsh is scenic and a good place to search for waterfowl and other wildlife. From the dike the trail continues as a two-track and remains that way until **Mile 5.6,** where the single track is marked by a blue blaze. This is another fast downhill run through a predominately hardwood forest. You cross several two-track forest roads along the way, but the blue markings will keep you on the trail.

After passing through a couple of open meadows, the trail reaches the pavement of 118th Avenue at **Mile 6.5**. On the other side of the road is Post J. You can head west here to return to the trailhead via Post H or continue the ride by heading left. The trail quickly dips onto 44th Street, a dirt road, and then back into the woods where it enters the dayuse area of Pine Point Campground and heads south. You skirt the campground itself, but it's easy to swing through it in order to use picnic tables, vault toilets or water pump.

From the campground the trail follows a powerline along a very hilly and sandy course. *Be careful here!* At **Mile 7.8** you re-cross 44th Street and at **Mile 8.2** you arrive at Post K. At this point the blue blazes direct you onto 116th Avenue and you follow the dirt road as it descends sharply to cross Swan Creek. You pass a posted trailhead for the Swan Creek Trail (for hikers only) and then make a steep climb up 116th Avenue away from the creek.

At the top, the road swings sharply north, but the route continues west through a parking area, past a locked gate and to Post L, reached at **Mile 8.6**.

You have a choice at this junction for the last leg to the trailhead. Head to Post M for a predominately forested ride that passes Post P and reaches the trailhead in 3.4 miles.

For a shorter route, make the sharp descent at Post L into the open field that is marked in the middle by a trail post. On the other side of the field you enter the woods for a pleasant stretch of single track and then arrive at Post P at Mile 10. In the remaining half mile the trail heads north to Post A at the refuge headquarters. From here you cross 118th Avenue and head a short ways up 46th Street to the trailhead parking area.

A biker heads towards the Jackson Hole-Whitford Lake Loops from the Red Loop of the Fort Custer Recreation Area. The trail bridge was installed in 1996 by the Southwest Chapter of the Michigan Mountain Bike Association.

Fort Custer Recreation Area

County: Kalamazoo
Total Mileage: 14.3 mile
Terrain: Wooded hills, some two track roads and open fields
Fees: Daily vehicle entry fee or annual state park pass
Difficulty: Easy to strenuous

Fort Custer Recreation Area is where the U.S. Army used to play army. It was a training and war games facility until the state Department of Natural Resources acquired it in 1971. Now the Fort is a place where people can play and recreate. And what a playground it is!

The 3,000-acre state park unit contains an abandoned town and former railroad and vehicle beds, all of which were used to form an extensive and interesting trail system for mountain bikers. Two trail systems have been designed and built since 1993. The 6.6-mile Green Loop, which uses letters (A,B,C,D,E, etc.) to guide you, is a combination of single track and stretches of old road that lace the park's interior. The route was designed as a slower, more scenic ride that winds around Eagle Lake and includes two shallow water

crossings and even a small waterfall. It can be handled by most novice riders, who are prepared to hop off their bike now and then.

The 7.7-mile Red Loop uses numbers (1, 2, 3) and is a masterpiece in trail design; a route that is challenging to iron-butted bikers, who ride every weekend, yet can be enjoyed by those just entering the sport. This was accomplished by using the former streets and rail beds to allow beginners and intermediate riders to easily bypass all the difficult stretches which are clearly marked and posted.

The trails are open year round for mountain biking. Some of the single track sections on the expert loop, however, are very sensitive to poor weather conditions. Riding in wet or muddy conditions may extenuate trail impact. The Southwest Chapter of the Michigan Mountain Biking Association, which built and maintains the trail system, recommends that if your tires are leaving ruts in the mud on the single-track ride only on the two-track roads until conditions dry out.

There are no facilities at trailhead but picnic areas, a beach and campground exist elsewhere in the recreation area.

Getting There: The entrance to Fort Custer Recreation Area is on M-96, 8 miles west of Battle Creek, just across the Kalamazoo River from Augusta.

Information: Contact Fort Custer Recreation Area, 5163 Fort Custer Dr., Augusta, MI 49012; ☎ (616) 731-4200. For a map of the bike trails contact the Michigan Mountain Biking Association at ☎ (616) 785-0120.

Green Loop
Distance: 6.6 miles
Trail: Single track and two-track
Direction: Counter clockwise
From the trailhead it's a short ride to Post 1, where the Red Loop heads west and the Green Loop heads south. Both trails end up back at the parking area. The Green Loop starts at Post A

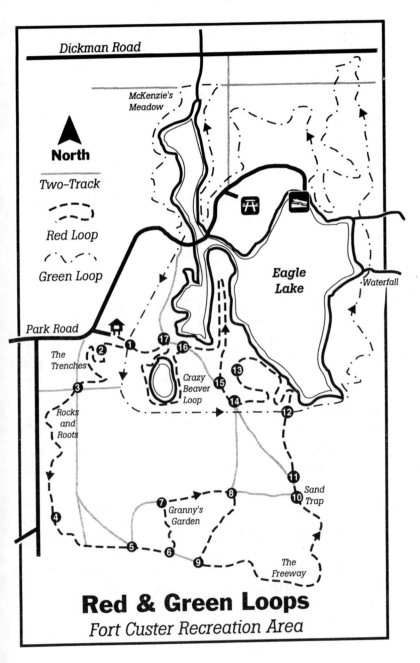

North

Two-Track

Red Loop

Green Loop

Dickman Road

McKenzie's Meadow

Eagle Lake

Waterfall

Park Road

The Trenches

Rocks and Roots

Crazy Beaver Loop

Granny's Garden

Sand Trap

The Freeway

Red & Green Loops
Fort Custer Recreation Area

as a two-track and within a quarter mile passes Post B, the intersection of an old army road. Post C marks where the Red Loop crosses the trail and at Post D, reached at **Mile 1**, the Green Loop becomes a single track.

Once on the single track, you begin to climb a very sharp, but short switchback. Traction is not a problem in dry weather, but it is a fairly technical climb and early use of a low gear with help you successfully reach the top.

At **Mile 2.4** is the first water-crossing. You'll drop down a steep bank into a creek, which usually has a depth of a foot or less in the summer, and then climb out on to the opposite steep bank. The banks have been reinforced to accommodate bike traffic and provide fairly good traction. The creek runs west to Eagle Lake over a small waterfall. Take a moment to park your bike off the trail and walk down to the cascade, the only one near a mountain bike trail in southern Michigan.

Less than a quarter mile along the trail is the second water crossing. Again the water is not deep, but the banks on both sides are steep plus there is a log that you must clear as you ride through the creek. This will surely test your technical riding skills if you want to avoid "swimming with the fishes."

The single track moves into some classic southern Michigan forested terrain as it heads north away from Eagle Lake to Post E, reached at **Mile 2.8**. The trail then returns to the lake at Post F at **Mile 3.8**, where nearby is a boat launch for Eagle Lake. For those who are over extended here, the launch area allows you to head back to the trailhead by riding the paved park road.

After passing through an open field that is dotted with spruce trees and wildflowers in the summer, you continue on the single track towards Post G, reached at **Mile 5.2**. Just before the post, the trail swings near the site of a classic beaver dam and lodge in the middle of a pond. The dam is only 50 yards off the trail, but in the summer the foliage is so thick it's hard to reach. In the spring and fall you'll be able to get off your bike and get a view of the dam without too much bushwhacking.

From Post G to Post H, there is a lot of winding single track with a few short, but technical climbs. Post H is passed just beyond **Mile 6** and from there the route uses a former road that heads straight back to the trailhead. At the end, you can call it a ride or start the second half of the adventure on the Red Loop.

Red loop

Distance: 7.7 miles
Trail: Single track and two-track
Direction: Counter clockwise

The first sections of the Red Loop are as close to riding a roller-coaster on a bike as you'll find anywhere. This roller coaster ride is the result of the military history on the area. In less than a mile, from Post 1 to Post 3, you'll be dropping down and up the sides of the Trenches (also called whoop-de-doos by many). Originally built buy the U.S. Army as training ditches, the Trenches now weave bikers back and forth along the rounded sides of the narrow troughs. You can take the whoop-de-doos at the speed you're comfortable with, but the faster you go, the more fun they are.

At Post 3, four two-track roads intersect at the trail, but the single track continues south and is well posted. Many riders exit the Red Loop at Post 3 and head back to the trailhead via the two-track roads to enjoy the Trenches all over again. Remember *the Red Loop (and Green Loop) are one-way, do not backtrack along them!*

The segment from Post 3 to Post 4 is moderately difficult due to roots and rocks in the trail. Just before reaching the junction you break out of the woods into an abandoned gravel pit. Post 4, reached at **Mile 1.4**, marks the spur that heads west (right) to loops around Jackson Hole and Whitford Lake after crossing a new trail bridge.

The Red Loop continues east (left) into some larger hills named creatively, First Hill and Second Hill. First Hill is a short climb with a long descent, Second Hill is the longest and steepest climb you will faced in the ride. The trail moves through a field and passes

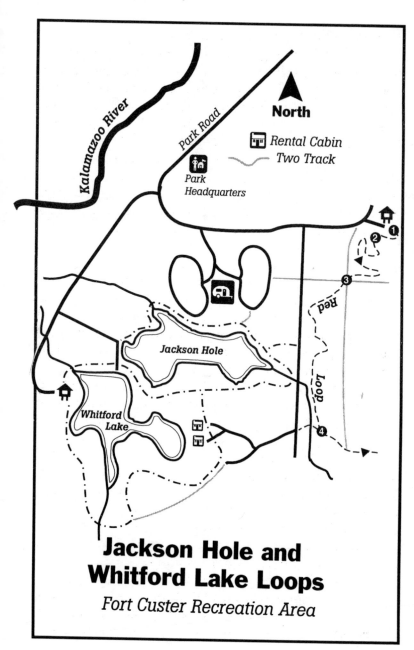

Jackson Hole and Whitford Lake Loops

Fort Custer Recreation Area

Post 5 and then Post 6 just beyond **Mile 2**.

Post 6 marks the segment called "Granny's Garden." Heading north at the intersection, is a very technical and strenuous section of trail where even intermediate riders will be thoroughly tested just to stay on their bikes. Beginners and others, whose bike skills are not up to speed, should bypass Granny's Garden by heading east at Post 6 and ride directly to Post 9.

About all that can be said about Granny's Garden is that you will encounter numerous tight, twisting, root and rock-filled hills and very, very tight and twisting downhills. Walking parts of this section is advised if your bike is not in top-functioning condition or your bike-handling skills unpolished.

By riding through the Garden, Post 9 is reached at **Mile 3.2** mile, where the trail enters "The Freeway" segment. Compared to Granny's Garden, it feels like you're going 100 mph because the trail is wide open and straight. This is where you can cruise. Be prepared as you approach Post 10, at **Mile 4.4**. Called the Sand Trap, it's an area at the bottom of a hill full of loose sand. If you're not paying attention, you'll do a close inspection of the Sand Trap via a header over your bars.

At **Mile 4.7** you reach Post 12 that marks where the Green Loop crosses the Red Loop from west. Post 12 is also the start of the Red Loop section known as the "Amusement Park", one of the first sections of single track built in the park. It winds and meanders towards Eagle Lake and then swings west to Post 13 and Post 14 at **Mile 5.9**. From Post 14 you head northwest to Post 15 where you begin a loop along Eagle Lake's most prominent peninsula. For more than a half mile, until reaching Post 16 at **Mile 6.5**, you are almost in constant view of water in this scenic stretch. At Post 15 you can take the two-track road northwest to Post 16 to eliminate a mile from the ride.

Post 16 marks a section know as the Crazy Beaver Loop, which winds south around a small lake. The lake has no stream feeding into it, but a beaver has built a lodge there anyway. What a crazy beaver! The first half of this loop is a ride above the lily pad-covered pond. You then make a rapid descent and enter the second half, which resembles the The Trenches between Post 2 and Post 3.

Crazy Beaver Loop is not as difficult as Granny's Garden, but you can bypass it by continuing on the two-track road to Post 17, **Mile 7.3** on the loop. From Post 17 the remaining half mile to trailhead is an easy ride west, passing Post 1 along the way.

Jackson Hole and Whitford Lake Loops

Distance: 5 miles
Trail: Single track
Direction: Counter clockwise

There are multi-use trails that skirt Jackson Hole, Whitford and Lawler Lakes in the Fort Custer Recreation Area. Presently mountain biking has not been restricted on these trails, but it is not recommended. The park's campground is located on Jackson Lake which contributes to large amount of pedestrian traffic on these trails in the way of hikers, campers and families. Nor are the Jackson Hole, Whitford and Lawler Lakes routes marked nearly as well as the Green and Red Loops.

If you do choose to ride these loops please do so with extreme caution and don't ride any faster than you can walk. You can access them from the campground, the park boat launch area that services both Jackson, Whitford and Lawler Lakes and Post 4 of the Red Loop. The post marks where a spur heads west, crosses a bridge over the stream from Jackson Hole and continues on the access road to the park's rental cabins. The Whitford and Lawler Lakes Loop, a 3-mile ride, passes through the parking areas of the cabins. The Jackson Hole Loop is a 2-mile route around the lake.

It's better to ride the Red and Green Loops if you can, especially if you are intent is speed or a non-stop workout on your bike. In any case, designation of the Lakes loop may change at any time, so check with the park manager or the MMBA for further information.

Kellogg Forest

County: Kalamazoo
Total Mileage: 10 miles
Terrain: Wooded hills
Fees: None
Difficulty: Moderate to strenuous

W.K. Kellogg Experimental Forest, or simply Kellogg Forest as most people refer to it, is a 700-acre tract in the northwest corner of Kalamazoo County and only a short drive from Fort Custer Recreation Area.

One of 14 field research facilities operated by Michigan State University, the forest was established in 1931 on 283 acres of worn-out farmland in an effort to study reforestation. Today the hilly preserve is almost totally wooded and is one of the premier research forests in the nation.

The area is also open to public recreation from 8 a.m. to 8 p.m. daily with the main activities being hiking, picnicing, fishing Augusta Creek, and driving the 2.5-mile Lemmien Loop Road, where visitors can learn to identify different species of trees. In the winter, the trails are open to cross country skiing. Hunting is permitted in the fall and the maple sugar cabin is operated every spring.

Kellogg Forest is split in the middle by 42nd

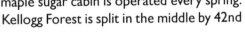

Situated near the office of Kellogg Forest is a "Big Wheel," left over from the days of lumberjacks and logging camps.

Street and mountain biking is permitted on the west side. Occupying about a third of the tract, the west side is a rolling terrain of tree plantations and a few open fields crisscrossed by roughly 10 miles of short trails, two-tracks and mowed lanes. Nothing is posted, no direction of travel has been established, no riding loop has been identified. You pretty much go in any direction you want, the trails are that numerous.

If you would rather follow a well marked loop with numbered posts that correspond to a map, then head south to the Fort Custer Recreation Area. But Kellogg Forest can be fun for those who just like to play with their bikes over a series of climbs and descents along trails that go every which way. Don't worry about getting lost, the area isn't that big. Ride a half mile in any direction and you'll come to the fences or roads that border it.

On the east side of 42nd Street is the main entrance to the forest and leads to the office, parking area, modern bathrooms and water. There are several gates to the west side along 42nd Street, but most bikers park near the office and use the one that is almost directly across the road from the main entrance.

Getting There: From I-94, depart at exit 85 and head north to pick up M-96. Follow M-96 east into Galesburg and stay on the state highway as it heads northeast 10 miles to Augusta. At the main four corners in Augusta, turn left on Webster Road. This becomes 42nd Street out of town and within 2 miles you reach the main entrance of the forest.

Information: Contact the W.K. Kellogg Experimental Forest 7060 N. 42nd St., Augusta, MI 49012; ☎ (616) 731-4597. The office is open only 9 a.m. to 1 p.m. but outside of it there is a map box for the trail system in the forest.

Kellogg Forest

Trail: two-tracks and mowed lanes
Direction: None

No attempt will be made to describe a route here as there are too many trails and two-tracks extending through the forest. The best way to explore the area the first time is to ride along the perimeter of the tract to get a sense of direction and then cut across the middle at will to return to the gate. Keep in mind the short distances of the trails in this half of the tract. If you follow the entire perimeter as close to the border fence as possible, that would still only be a 2.5-mile ride.

At the gate across from the main entrance, you can go either north (right) or south (left) along a dirt two-track. By heading south and staying left at every junction, you skirt the southern half

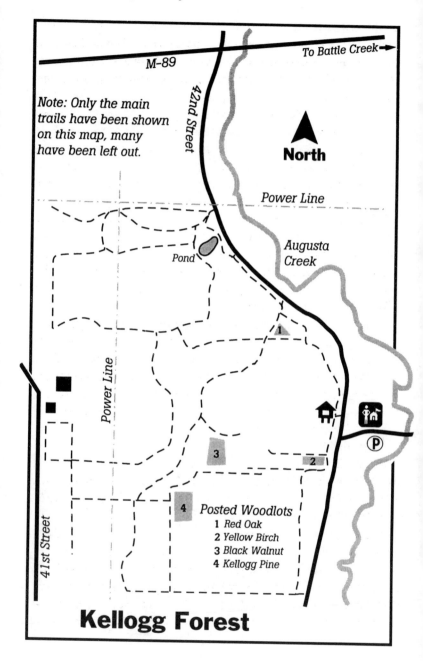

Note: Only the main trails have been shown on this map, many have been left out.

M-89

To Battle Creek

42nd Street

North

Power Line

Pond

Augusta Creek

1

Power Line

3

2

41st Street

4

Posted Woodlots
1 Red Oak
2 Yellow Birch
3 Black Walnut
4 Kellogg Pine

Kellogg Forest

of the tract. In this direction, the two-track quickly becomes a mowed grassy lane that passes a posted stand of Yellow Birch and then makes a sharp turn to the west. Continue straight on the trail and you'll climb a hill into an open meadow, roughly the center of the tract.

If you turn left instead of climbing the hill, the trail winds through the woods above paved 42nd Street. In a half mile from the gate you make another sharp turn west, with the border fence on one side and the junctions to a half dozen trails on other. It's a gradual climb for the next quarter mile until you top off at a spot where the mowed lane makes a sharp turn north (right).

The lane skirts a pine plantation and then comes to a junction of three trails, two to the right and one to the left. Head left and you make a quick climb and end at the fence along the west side, where you can see a couple of homes. Heading north (right) quickly brings you to some buildings and a farm house on the property, a 1.3-mile ride from the gate.

Back at the gate across from the main entrance, if you veer right and stay right, you will skirt the northern half of the tract, the portion with the steepest hills. You make an immediate climb into the woods from the gate and descend to a V-intersection. Hang right and you breakout at a clearing and a tree plantations. One of the stands is posted as Red Oak and a well-defined trail skirts it and enters the natural woods for the center of the tract.

Hang left and follow the grassy lane along 42nd Street and you'll quickly reach a trail that climbs a small rise to one end of a scenic little pond. You then enter a pine plantation of older trees and come to a V-intersection. Follow either route here and you'll soon be climbing hills. The tallest one is reached by turning right and staying along the perimeter of the track where you follow a powerline right-a-way over a pair of steep hills. The second one puts you at the northwest corner of the tract, a mile ride from the gate, where a fence prevents you from going any further west. Backtrack and head south along the first few junctions for more climbs or an attempt to reach the other half of the forest.

At Yankee Springs Recreation Area, one of the most popular biking areas in Western Michigan, even the park rangers use mountain bikes to patrol the trails and campgrounds.

Yankee Springs Recreation Area

County: Barry
Total Mileage: 12.7 miles
Terrain: Wooded Hills
Fees: Daily vehicle entry permit or annual state park pass
Difficulty: Easy to strenuous

Yankee Springs Recreation Area is the site of the first multiuse trail in Southwestern Michigan built after mountain biking took off in the early 1990s. Located in the Deep Lake portion of the state park unit, the system was named the Cramer/Lawson Trail and reflects the distinct characteristics of the two mountain bikers who designed it.

Mark Cramer and Bob Lawson, who live near the recreation area, built the trail on the invitation of the park staff. In the world of mountain biking, Cramer was an avid cross country rider while Lawson, at the time, was on his way to national recognition as a trials rider. If you look closely you can see their influence on the trails. Cramer's sections often tend to be straight and fast with big sweeping turns and long climbs on the hills. Lawson's segments, near the end of the ride, are tight, twist-

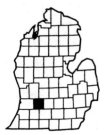

ing and often laid out over obstacles, showing the predisposition towards his trials riding background (why go around the log or rock when you can go over it!).

The trailhead is located at the Deep Lake Campground on the east side of the 5,200-acre recreation area. Yankee Springs attracts 750,000 visitors annually, but the vast majority are attracted to Gun Lake with its beach, dayuse area and modern campground. Still, during the summer, Deep Lake often reaches full capacity due to the increase of mountain bikers and a new parking lot has been built to accommodate them. Probably the most popular mountain biking area in western Michigan, you can expect changes to accomodate the heavy traffic and preserve the trail for the future.

The Cramer/Lawson Trail System consists of a 2-mile loop near the parking lot for beginners and an 11-mile route that is recommended for intermediate and advanced riders.

Facilities at Deep Lake include vault toilets and a water pump along with the rustic campsites. The trails are open year round for mountain bikers. But some sections on the expert loops are very sensitive to poor weather conditions. Riding in the wet or muddy conditions of late March and early April will impact the trail. Also keep in mind that some stretches are used by both bikers and hikers.

Getting There: From US-131, depart at exit 61 and head east on County Road A42 for 8 miles to the park entrance. From there follow Gun Lake Road (CR-430) through the middle of the park and then turn north on Yankee Springs Road to the entrance of Deep Lake Campground.

The mountain bike staging area and the beginner's loop are on the north side of the gravel access road to the campground. The longer intermediate and expert trail ends on the south side.

Information: Contact Yankee Springs Recreation Area, 2104 Gun Lake Rd., Middeville, MI 49333 ☎ (616) 795-9081.

A mountain biker at the end of long race. Races are held annually at Yankee Springs Recreation Area.

Cramer/Lawson Trail
Beginner's Loop

Distance: 2 miles
Trail: Single track
Direction: Counter clockwise (expect directional changes in the future)

In the mountain bike staging area, you can see where the 2-mile Beginner's Loop ends at the northwest side of the parking lot. Just across the access road is where the Expert Loop begins. To ride the Beginner's Loop, follow the access road to the entrance. The trailhead is on the north side.

The short loop is clearly marked and rolls gently through hardwoods and pines ending up in the parking lot. At the half-mile mark, you come to a fork in the trail (so bring dinner!), where it's possible to get a feel of what the expert portion of the trail is like. Though the fork is not marked, if you go left (west) you'll descend a very steep, but short, slope into a valley of loose dirt, returning via a short bank of rock and gravel on the other side. If you go straight at the fork you'll stay at the top of the bank and avoid this technical spur.

This spur is the only real variation in the trail. The rest gently rolls along for 1.5 miles to eventually skirt the rustic sites of the Deep Lake Campground and return to the staging area.

Expert Loop

Distance: 11 miles
Trail: Single track
Direction: Counter clockwise (expect directional changes in the future)

The Expert Loop begins just south of the staging area, where a trail map is posted and is considered Post 1. The trail begins by descending a half dozen flexible waterbars which help stabilize the first of several sandy segments of the trail.

The route heads south and at **Mile 0.6** descends sharply to cross a bridge over(expect directional changes in the future)a creek from Deep Lake before entering a segment of rolling woods for almost 2 miles. There are climbs and descents, but none particularly hard or technical.

At **Mile 2.5**, you arrive at Post 2, a confusing intersection of several trails and Hart and Basset Lake roads. The dirt roads are separated from the trails by a guard rail while the mountain bike route is clearly marked, including a map on Post 2. By heading east a mile on Hart Road you reach paved Yankee Springs Road, a half mile north of the Deep Lake Campground entrance.

From Post 2, it's a quarter mile ride to Post 2a, which marks a crossover spur that allows you to begin heading back and skip

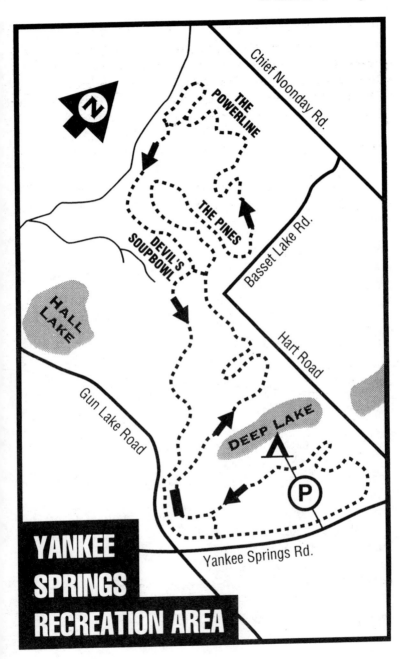

THE POWERLINE

THE PINES

DEVIL'S SOUPBOWL

HALL LAKE

DEEP LAKE

Chief Noonday Rd.

Basset Lake Rd.

Hart Road

Gun Lake Road

Yankee Springs Rd.

YANKEE SPRINGS RECREATION AREA

the most challenging segments of this mountain bike system. Continuing on the main trail, you'll gently climb a ridge for a mile and then ride across a series of moraines with very steep sides. You'll need your best pair of legs to avoid walking here. It's important to know when and how to brake properly to avoid skidding or even sliding off the trail and down the side of the moraines. In short, take it easy on this difficult stretch. In fact, the slower and more controlled you are, the better you'll appreciate how a mile-high glacier carved this terrain more than 10,000 years ago.

At **Mile 4**, the trail arrives at Post 2b, an emergency access point for park rangers, and then passes through a pine tree plantation before swinging past Basset Lake Road for the second time at **Mile 4.6**. If you're riding in July, you're in for a treat at this spot. The wildberries by the hundreds should be ripening on the bushes and you could go away with your riding gloves stained black, but your sweet tooth satisfied.

From Basset Lake Road, the trail continues west along a segment with Cramer's signature on it. You'll be tackling some very big hills with sweeping high bank turns and plenty of straight shots to keep your feet cranking. Ride this stretch carefully! Due to the increased use of the trail the surface can be very rough and unstable at times. This section will test anybody's endurance level and their skill to ride off-road, not to mention their bike's worthiness. *Take it slow!*

Post 3 is reached at **Mile 6.2**, and some riders will be thankful to know they can take a crossover spur at this post to begin the return to Deep Lake and reduce the ride by a little more than a mile.

The main trail, however, uses a series of sharp turns and switchbacks to descend a long hill, only to bottom out and resume climbing towards what some locals call "Lookout Hill," reached near **Mile 7**. The name is well deserved since in the early spring or late fall, the highpoint provides a commanding view of the surrounding farmland. It also serves as a great "halfway point" (well almost) for a break. The hill is easy to identify by the USGS survey marker at the top.

You descend Lookout Hill and at **Mile 8.2** pass the crossover spur from Post 2a as well as pass near Devil's Soup Bowl, a steep sided depression more than a 100 feet deep. The almost bottomless pit may appear to have been scooped out by a backhoe, but is another sign of the glacial activity that molded this region of the state. *There is no mountain biking in or around Devil's Soup Bowl,* but it is well worth your time to walk around it to enjoy what a few thousand years of glacial erosion can do.

Post 3a, another emergency access point, is reached at **Mile 8.6** and after descending a rock-filled slope the trail becomes a much more mellow ride. You break out into a pleasant meadow near **Mile 9.5** and then skirt paved Gun Lake Road briefly. The trail uses a culvert to cross the stream from Deep Lake and finally arrives at Post 4a at **Mile 10**.

The final mile-leg of the loop is a considerably harder stretch thanks to Lawson. It features numerous short descents and climbs out of ravines along with riding off-camber, over logs and rocks along a narrow, winding trail.

You'll find yourself going a lot slower to negotiate the turns and having to crank harder and in lower gears to get up the short, steep hills. Once you "pass Lawson's trial," you'll emerge at the Deep Lake Campground access road at **Mile 11**. At this point, you can continue directly on the two-mile Beginner's Loop across the road, or head west a few hundred yards to the staging area. The Beginner's Loop makes a nice cool down after the Expert Loop.

Lake
Michigan

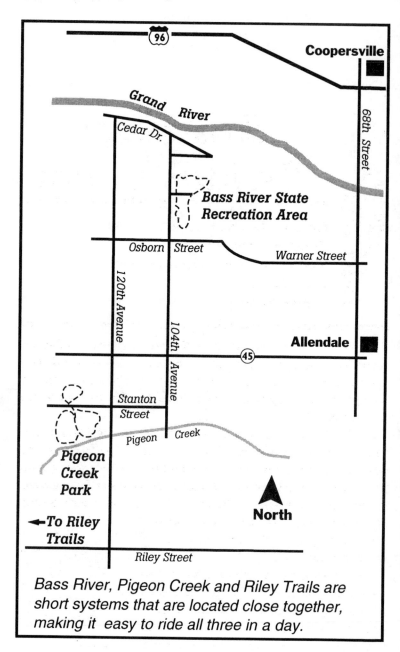

Bass River, Pigeon Creek and Riley Trails are short systems that are located close together, making it easy to ride all three in a day.

Bass River
Recreation Area

County: Ottawa County
Total Mileage: 3.5 miles
Terrain: Hardwood and pine forest
Fees: None
Difficulty: Easy

The trail system at Bass River Recreation Area is a flat but twisty 3.5-mile loop through the woods that most mountain bikers can cover in 30 minutes or less. When compared to Yankee Springs or Fort Custer Recreation Areas, Bass River hardly seems worth mentioning.

On the other hand, the state Department of Natural Resources has invited organizations interested in the area to help develop it and this eventually could lead to a 12-mile trail system for mountain bikers, hikers and cross country skiers. Future plans for the recreation area might also include a boat launch on the Bass River, which flows into the Grand River, and a campground. Presently, there are no facilities in the park.

An interesting adventure is to combine Bass River with several other limited trail systems in the area for a fun day of riding. The state recreation area is less than 10 miles from both Pigeon Creek County Park and Hofma

Park and 15 miles from Riley Street Park.

Families and beginners can load their bikes on their car and trail hop from one park to another, stopping in between rides for food and refreshments. By driving between trailheads, most bikers can cover all four trails in a day. More experienced bikers will want to leave their cars at one of the trailheads and ride their bike from park to park, mixing trail riding with an on-road adventure. An Ottawa County map would reveal the road routes between the parks and give you an idea of how much mileage you would pile up for the day.

Getting There: From US-31, head east on M-45 (Lake Michigan Drive) for 7 miles to 104th Avenue, where you turn north. Within 2.2 miles, look for a gravel road with a swing gate on east side of 104th Avenue. Driving into the recreation area is prohibited so leave your vehicle on the side of the park road near the entrance. The trail runs north to south across the park road.

Information: Contact the West Michigan Chapter of the Michigan Mountain Bike Association at ☎ (616) 785-0120.

Bass River Recreation Area
Distance: 3.5 miles
Trail: Single track, two-track and gravel roads
Direction: Counter clockwise

The Bass River Trail is firm and for the most part winds through hardwood and pine forests. The best route is to head south from the park road just after entering the state recreation area.

The trail is marked here and loops through the woods until **Mile 0.7** where it comes to a fence and horse trail that runs east-to-west. At this point the trail curves east and then north, reaching the park road at **Mile 1.5**. Follow the gravel road east briefly and then turn northeast (left) onto another gravel road.

This one turns into a two-track and then at **Mile 1.7** the single track resumes by heading northwest back into the woods. Eventually, it curves its way south to skirt 104th Avenue and returns to the park road at **Mile 3.5**.

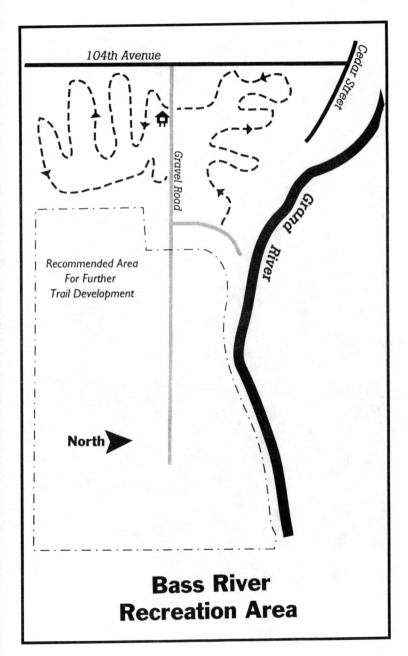

104th Avenue

Cedar Street

Gravel Road

Grand River

Recommended Area
For Further
Trail Development

North

Bass River
Recreation Area

The trail system at Pigeon Creek County Park swings includes numerous wetlands that in the spring come alive with colorful patches of marsh marigold and other wildflowers.

Pigeon Creek County Park

County: Ottawa
Total Mileage: 6.3 miles
Terrain: Woods, Pigeon Creek, some hills
Fees: None
Difficulty: Easy

Located between Muskegon and Holland, Pigeon Creek is 432 acres of dedicated park land and adjoining county land that was redeveloped in 1996, thanks in part to a grant from the Michigan Natural Resources Trust Fund.

A new entrance and parking area were developed, a group campground was installed and a warming lodge\picnic shelter was built. But all these amenities pale when compared to the nine-mile trail system that capture the interest of cross country skiers in the winter and mountain bikers in the summer.

Because of the sandy soil and dune environment of Ottawa County, Pigeon Creek is the only county park to cater to mountain bikers. More than six miles of trail is open to bikers of which three-quarters is a well-packed surface in the woods. The rest involves sand or loose soil, but in these sections a gravel bed has been applied to the trail in an effort to combat the impact of fat-tire bicycles. Bikers also share the trails with hikers while equestrians have their own trail system within the park.

Pigeon Creek is not a technical ride because most of the trails are old two-tracks and, except for a couple of steep hills, it is generally a level trail system that is easy to follow. But not being technical doesn't mean the trails aren't enjoyable, especially to beginners, families and anybody who goes mountain biking to soak in the natural setting. Pigeon Creek is well designed for that as there are several places to stop at observation decks, benches and overlooks to enjoy the wetlands, wildflowers or the clear-running creek itself.

The trail system is divided into two sections. A 2-mile loop through a red pine plantation is on the north side of Stanton Road. But the more interesting stretches are on the south side where you have a half dozen loop combinations to choose from with the outside trails forming the longest one, a 2.7-mile ride. The ride described here is a combination of that loop with a 2-mile segment on the north side of the road.

Getting There: From Grand Rapids head west on M-45 and in 15 miles turn south on 120th Avenue. Turn west on Stanton and the park entrance is reached in less than a mile.

Information: Contact the Ottawa County Parks and Recreation Commission, 414 Washington St., Grand Haven, MI 49417; ☎ (616) 846-8117.

Pigeon Creek County Park

Distance: 4.7 Miles
Trail: Two-track
Direction: Counter clockwise

The main entrance is on the south side of the Stanton Road and features a parking lot, vault toilets and picnic facilities, as well

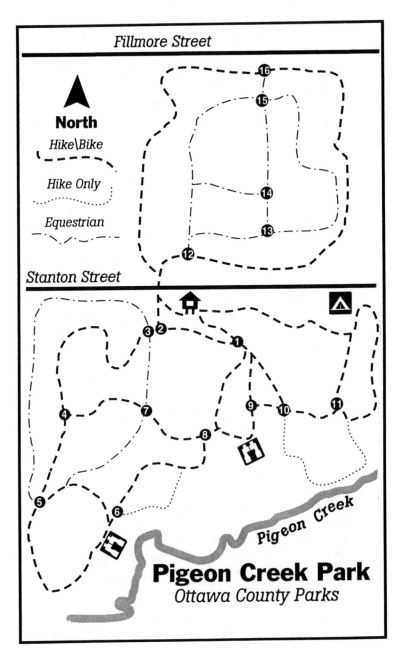

Lake Michigan

North

Hike\Bike

Hike Only

Equestrian

Fillmore Street

Stanton Street

Pigeon Creek

Pigeon Creek Park
Ottawa County Parks

the trailhead. On the north side of the road is the parking area and trailhead for equestrians.

The trail begins by climbing up a partially open dune where at the top is the park's warming hut/picnic shelter. Riders in the middle of a hot summer must think this is what it's like to bike in the Sahara Dessert because sand will be blowing into your ears and gears. From the top of the dune, Post 1, you head right and descend to Post 2, where a two-way trail takes you across Stanton Road to the north half of the park.

On the north side of Stanton, continue in a counter clockwise direction and within a few hundred yards arrive at Post 12. Continue straight ahead as the other route is an equestrian's trail. The trail on this side of the road is a 2-mile loop that in the first half stays in a pine plantation and then after Post 16 moves into a younger growth of aspen and beech for a spell. Part of the trail is hard pack forest tract, the rest of it is soft sand in which cycling can be an effort.

At **Mile 2.4**, you recross Stanton Road and quickly arrive at Post 2. Take a right to reach Post 3 (but avoid the equestrian's trail) and enter the green canopy of a hardwood forest. The unique aspect of this park is its many different microclimates, with this forest being just one. It's an easy and winding ride past Post 4 to Post 5 at **Mile 3.2**, the start of the Ridge Loop segment. Here you climb gently to within the view of a dirt road and then descend the first of two steep hills in the system.

The trail swings northeast and passes an observation deck before reaching Post 6. Take time to walk out on the deck which cuts through a marsh to the edge of Pigeon Creek. Just beyond Post 6 you pass the first of two *Hiking Only* segments, Hemlock Path, which drops down off the high ground. Just beyond the return of this trail is a short spur that leads to benches and an overlook on a low bluff of the surrounding marshes. Nice spot to take a break.

Post 8 is reached at **Mile 4** and Post 9 is just a hundred yards down the trail, where you are faced with the steepest hill of the system. You bottom out at Post 10 where the second *Hiker's Only* trail departs to the left. This half-mile loop skirts the Pigeon River, features a few benches and again is well worth the time to leave the bike behind.

Post 11 is reached at **Mile 6.5** and from here you have two options to return to the trailhead. The shortest route is a half mile ride, the other is Red Pine Loop, a slightly longer ride through a red pine plantation. Follow this loop and you pass the group campground on the way back and emerge at the east side of the parking area for a 4.7-mile ride.

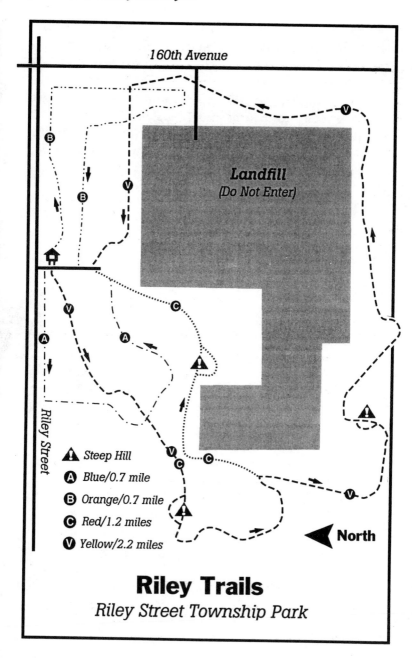

160th Avenue

Landfill
(Do Not Enter)

Riley Street

⚠ *Steep Hill*

Ⓐ *Blue/0.7 mile*

Ⓑ *Orange/0.7 mile*

Ⓒ *Red/1.2 miles*

Ⓥ *Yellow/2.2 miles*

◀ **North**

Riley Trails
Riley Street Township Park

Riley Street Park

County: Ottawa County
Total Mileage: 5 miles
Terrain: Hardwood and pine forests, some hills
Fees: none
Difficulty: Easy

Riley Street Park is not a trail you'd pick as a mountain bike adventure. Even if you lived down the street, you would probably shrug your shoulders when asked about riding in the park and simply say, "It's there, no big deal". But for many families in the Holland, Zeeland and Hudsonville areas, this park, with an old landfill in the middle, is ideal.

The 5-mile trail system is a great place for children and adults just entering the mountain bike world or locals looking for a quick ride. You can easily put together several segments for a three-mile excursion that is just challenging enough to be fun, but not too intimidating to new riders.

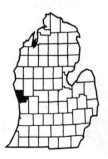

The trail is just northwest of Holland with the parking area and trailhead on the south side of Riley Street. The four main loops depart and return from either the parking lot or a short two-track road that departs south from here.

It's important to remember that there are a lot of crisscrossing spurs and unofficial side trails in the park that lead to dead-ends, fenced in areas and private property. The system was not laid out as part of contiguous whole, but rather as a progression of trail development, as more and more hikers and cross country skiers and mountain bikers used the area. Just finding your way around the park can sometimes be an adventure, but what mountain biking be without a few dead ends, right?

In general, the trails are identified by painted blazes or discs on the trees and marked well enough to follow, though at times, you might have to stop and ponder which way to go. It's hard to get lost, the park is not that big, and impossible to wander into the old landfill, that area is completely fenced in.

The longest loop is the 2.2-mile V trail, which skirts the landfill and is coded in yellow. This southern half of this loop is not recommended for mountain bikes because the area is extremely sandy, including a large open dune-like area. Extending off the V Loop is the C Loop (red), a 1.2-mile ride while the A Loop (blue) and B Loop (orange) are a pair of easy trails of less than a mile in length. These trails remain in the woods in the northern half of the park and have a considerably harder surface. The park is so near Lake Michigan, you have to expect some sandy stretches on all trails.

Riley Trails are open year-round to mountain biking except when there is adequate snow for cross country skiers in the winter. Remember the rule: "Four inches of snow; don't go on multiuse trails."

Getting There: The trail system is 5 miles west of US-31 and a mile from Lake Michigan. From US-31, depart at the Lakewood Road exit and head west for 4.5 miles and then turn north (right) on 160th Avenue for 1.5 miles. Turn west (left) onto Riley Street and within a half mile the parking area and trailhead is posted on the south side of the road.

Information: Contact Park Township, 52 152nd Ave., Holland, MI 49424; ☎ (616) 399-4520.

Riley Trails
Distance: 2.6 miles
Trail: Single track
Direction:

Of the many loop combinations at Riley Street Park, this is my favorite ride. From the parking lot, begin on Loop A as the trail heads west through the narrow rows of trees of a red pine plantation. At **Mile 0.4**, you make a short sandy ascent to arrive at the junction with V/C Loop. Continue on the V/C Loop by following the yellow/red blazes on the trees.

Within a quarter mile you'll come to a confusing spot where an unofficial spur crosses over to the second half of the C Loop. Look to the right here to continue following the yellow/red blazes. The trail quickly arrives at the first of several small hills in the park where there is a bypass, primarily meant for skiers.

You stay in the hardwood forest and at **Mile 1.2**, C and V Loops split. Head left on C Loop as the V Loop continues south into a wide open sandy area where the trail is poorly marked. C Loop heads east and within a quarter mile arrives at the steepest slope in the park. Even most beginners can survive this downhill run, but there is a bypass trail to the right though it's hard to see during the summer.

Eventually A Loop merges with C Loop and both end at the two-track road at **Mile 1.4**, just south of the parking lot. To continue this ride, head towards the parking lot to jump on the B Loop, marked by orange blazes that are so faded sometimes they look yellow. Bear right (east) on the B Loop and at **Mile 1.8** you'll be in view of 160th Avenue, the east boundary of the park.

The trail heads south here for a third of a mile to another two-track road that leads from 160th Avenue to the abandoned landfill. At this point the B Loop heads west then northwest to cross V Loop. This can be a confusing spot because the blazes of both trails are difficult to distinguish from each other. Either loop, however, will return you to the parking lot in a half mile along a wooded segment that is very level.

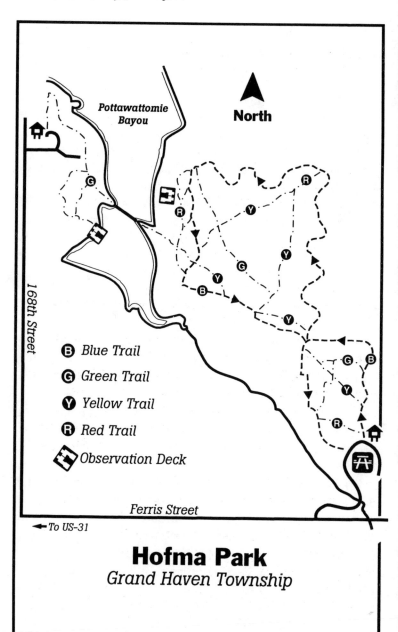

North

Pottawattomie Bayou

168th Street

B *Blue Trail*

G *Green Trail*

Y *Yellow Trail*

R *Red Trail*

Observation Deck

Ferris Street

← *To US-31*

Hofma Park
Grand Haven Township

Hofma Park

County: Ottawa
Total Mileage: 4.5 miles
Terrain: Flat, wooded preserve
Fees: None
Difficulty: Easy

If there was ever a place designed for children and their first time on a mountain bike, Hofma Park is the place. All the trails are wide and well marked. There are no climbs and very few sections with exposed roots and rocks. In the early spring and late fall, a family can have the trails to themselves. On such afternoons, Hofma Park is a non-threatening place to ride, making it ideal for beginners, especially children, to enjoy a roll through the woods.

At the Ferris Street trailhead, there is a picnic area with bathrooms, water, an elaborate play area and a large trail map. You can enter the trail system just to the north of this map for a counter clockwise ride through the park. The most user-friendly ride and the best marked loop is the Blue Trail. It follows the perimeter of the park, is well marked and makes a loop of 3.2 miles. There are several other trails, yellow, green and red, that criss-cross the interior of the property and make

for scenic additions to the Blue Trail.

Keep in mind that the trails extend through a dedicated natural area, making it extremely popular with hikers. The trails are also popular with cross country skiers and the Lake Michigan side of the state is renown for its early and sudden snow storms. Don't count on riding these trails after November. On the other hand, this area is closed to hunting so the park can provide you with an opportunity on your bike during the firearm deer season from Nov. 15-30.

Getting There: From US-31, 3 miles south of Grand Haven, turn east onto Ferris Street to reach the main park entrance on the north side of the road in 1.5 miles. There is also an entrance on the north side of the park off of Sleeper Street, a half mile east off of 168th Avenue.

Information: Contact Grand Haven Township Parks, 13300 168th Ave., Grand Haven, MI 49417; ☎ (616) 842-3515.

Blue Trail
Distance: 3.2 miles
Trail: Wide single track
Direction: Counter clockwise

From the display map, the Blue Trail heads into the woods, but quickly passes junctions with the Red, Yellow and Green trails. The beginning can be a little confusing, but the Blue Trail is well marked and easy to pick up at every intersection. Within a third of a mile you briefly parallel a subdivision that is separated from the park by a fence and a large trench. Several well used but non-authorized trails head east to the subdivision, but again blue posts keep you heading north on the designated loop.

The Blue Trail makes a sweeping curve west and at **Mile 0.6** there is a major junction with a bench and a map. There seems to be trails and color posts everywhere here. Take the first right and stay with the blue posts to avoid a segment of Yellow Trail, which cuts across to the northwest side of the park.

At this point the Blue Trail winds north through the woods and is marked by both posts and blue diamonds in the trees. At **Mile 1**, you pass a well-marked junction with the Red Trail that leads into the interior of the loop. In the next quarter mile, you'll also pass so called "feeder spurs" that head south to the Yellow Trail and more non-authorized trails heading north to a subdivision. The Blue Trail remains well posted and easy to spot.

You see a few more homes through the trees and then at **Mile 1.5** arrive at a junction with the Green Trail heading south (left) into the interior of the loop. In less than 100 yards a second junction pops up. Here the Blue Trail takes a sharp left to the south while the Red Trail extends towards the open water of Pottawattomie Bayou.

This section of the Red Trail follows the low bluffs above the bayou, passing an observation deck along the way. Not to be confused with the Potawatomi Trail near Ann Arbor (you East Siders!), Pottawattomie Bayou is a fantastic place to see a variety of both permanent and migrating waterfowl throughout the year.

Also off the Red Trail is a segment of the Yellow Trail that leads to a floating boardwalk across the bayou. On the other side is a short section of the Green Trail that leads to an observation tower. With a little bit of time and a set of binoculars, you can usually spot waterfowl either when *walking* your bike across the boardwalk or from one of the observation decks.

The Blue Trail, meanwhile, heads almost due south and in early spring and late fall you are rewarded with glimpses of the bayou through the trees. You pass several spurs that head west (right) toward the Red Trail and two junctions with the Yellow Trail. Just past **Mile 2**, the Red Trail returns and the Blue Trail veers hard to the left. More segments of the Yellow Trail are posted along this stretch of the Blue Trail and at **Mile 2.6** you return to the same intersection that was passed in the first half mile of the ride.

This time follow the blue posts to the right to complete this loop for a ride of 3.2 miles. You emerge at the park road just west of the trail map in the picnic area.

A mountain biker crosses an open meadow along the Pentwater Pathway. This state forest trail system is one of the closest to Southern Michigan, a mere hour's drive from Grand Rapids.

Pentwater Pathway

County: Oceana
Total Mileage: 7.4 miles
Terrain: Woods, rolling hills
Fees: None
Difficulty: Easy to moderate

State forest pathways, a 600-mile system scattered across Michigan's 3.9 million acres of state forest land, have always been popular destinations with mountain bikers ever since the sport exploded on the scene in the late 1980s.

The closest pathway to southern Michigan, not much more than an hour drive from Grand Rapids and even less from Muskegon, is Pentwater Pathway, located southeast of the popular resort town and only a mile from US-31. Despite its close-to-home location, the 7.4-mile trail system does not receive the heavy use most other state forest trails do.

Part of the reason is that Pentwater Pathway lacks the scenic beauty of the Sand Lakes Quiet Area, the steep hills of the Black Mountain Recreation Area or the mileage of the VASA. Still, you'll find Pentwater an uncrowded and well wooded trail. There are no cornfield-like red pine plantations here, rather the track winds through a beautiful mixed forest of maple, beech and spruce trees, some of impressive size. In the summer, the forest makes for a cool ride even on the hottest day. In early October, it's a magnificent blend of autumn colors and in the winter cross country skiers take over.

The trail system is a 6-mile single track loop with three cross-over spurs that allow you to shorten the route or avoid a particularly hilly stretch. The trail winds through a rolling terrain of low ridges. Novice riders ready to take their mountain biking skills to the next level can do so with the handful of challenging hills towards the end of the ride.

There are a number of old forest two-tracks that cross the pathway, but the trail is well marked at most intersections. The only thing to watch out for are the numerous sand traps at the bottom of many hills.

Getting There: From US-31, depart onto Business Route US-31 towards Pentwater and then head south on County Road B-15, which is posted with a "State Forest Pathway" sign. You immediately cross Pentwater Lake on Long Bridge and then continue south from B-15 on Wayne Avenue. After 1.5 miles turn west onto a posted sandy two-track, which passes through the pathway parking lot.

Information: Contact the Baldwin Forest Field Office, 1757, E. Hayes Rd, Shelby, MI 49455; ☎ (616) 861-5636.

Pentwater Pathway

Distance: 6 miles
Trail: Single track
Direction: Clockwise

From Wayne Avenue you follow a sandy two-track for a third of a mile, where it passes through the pathway parking lot though it's hard to tell. There is no trailhead, display map or even a pit toilet here, just a trail into the woods at the west end of the lot.

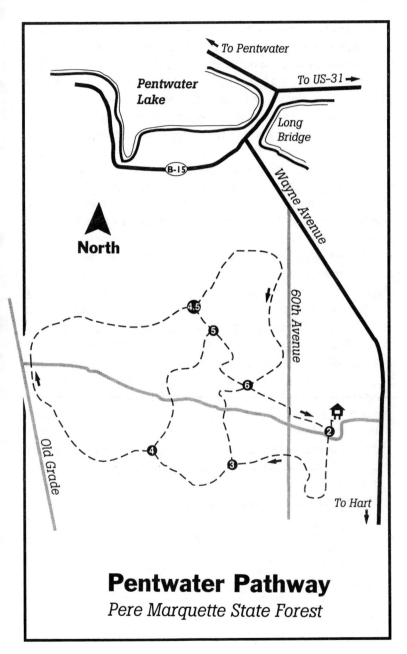

Pentwater Pathway
Pere Marquette State Forest

Follow the trail and in a quarter mile you will be reassured you're on the pathway as Post 2, complete with a trail map, pops up.

Head left and follow the loop in a clockwise direction. The trail quickly crosses a pair of old two-tracks and then follows the crest of a low, winding and wooded ridge. A couple of small meadows do break up the beauty of the forest and just past the second one, you cross 60th Avenue, a dirt road, and arrive at Post 3 at *Mile 1.2*.

Continue left for the outside loop, where you encounter a couple of small hills and a few more grassy openings in the woods. The riding remains fairly easy, however, and just before **Mile 2**, you arrive at Post 4 and another opportunity to follow a cross-over spur to shorten the trip.

The next leg to Post 4.5 begins with more gentle riding for the first mile through woods and meadows. Eventually you pedal right underneath an apple tree where it's easy to grab one if you're hungry, and then cross an old two-track near the intersection with Old Grade Road at **Mile 3**. On the other side, the trail enters an older stand of trees, featuring some very large hardwoods that are brilliant in October.

The top half of this loop is definitely more challenging than the bottom half. You cross three old two-tracks and then take on two large hills with the second one just before Post 4.5 at **Mile 4**. The segment from Post 4.5 to Post 6, obviously added after the original trail was built, is the most challenging stretch. Bypass it if you had problems with the last two hills.

The steepest hill is encountered just after passing Post 4.5. From there the trail remains a rolling ride for the next third-of-a-mile until you cross another old two-track. On the other side you are challenged with three more steep slopes followed by equally hard climbs. Except for the sand pits that seem to lie at the bottom of each descent, these downhill runs shouldn't overwhelm too many novice mountain bikers with experience riding single-track trails.

You reach Post 6 at **Mile 5.2** and from there it's an easy ride of less than a mile back to the parking lot.

Whiskey Creek

County: Mason
Total Mileage: 6.2 miles
Terrain: Wooded and hilly
Fees: Trail fee
Difficulty: Easy to strenuous

Of all the trails reviewed in this book, Whiskey Creek probably has the most remote location. Once you leave Hawley Road for Whiskey Creek Campground, you get the feeling you're headed somewhere deep in the woods. And you are, but for many of us that's what mountain biking is all about.

Don't confuse Whiskey Creek's remote location with rustic facilities. The campground has all the amenities you might want including modern campsites and a lodge with an indoor swimming pool, hot tub and restaurant. In addition to the 6.2-mile wooded trail system, which was upgraded and marked for mountain bikers in the spring of 1997, Whiskey Creek also stages several races annually.

Many other adventures are also possible as Whiskey Creek is surrounded by the Huron-Manistee National Forests. From the campground you can jump on the Michigan Cross Country Cycle Trail (CCC Trail), which is firm

enough to be ridden during wet times of the year. A portion of the motorcycle trail is used for the Deep Thaw Classic ride, an annual event every spring at Whiskey Creek. The Deep Thaw is a 25-mile ride and will eventually be a posted route for Whiskey Creek mountain bikers.

Within 10 miles of the campground is a trailhead for a portion of the North Country Trail (see Bowman Lake To Timber Creek ride in the North Country Trail section) or you can explore miles of two-track roads that wind through the national forest. In terms of biking opportunities, Whiskey Creek is flooded!

Getting There: From M-37, head west on US-10. Within 10 miles turn south on Walhalla Road, west on Hawley Rd and south on Woods Trail, a gravel road. Signs along Woods Trail will direct you to the lodge.

Information: Contact Whiskey Creek, 5080 Sippy Rd., Custer, MI 49405; ☎ (800) 792-7335.

Whiskey Creek

Distance: 6.2 miles
Trail: Single track
Direction: Counter clockwise

From the front of the lodge, head east to the trailhead of the 6.2-mile trail system. It's all within a mile of the campground and on a mix of single track and hiking/cross country ski trails that are marked by red signs.

After skirting an abandoned snowmobile track and the campground, the trail departs into the woods. At **Mile 2.2**, you make two hard rights that put you on some tight single track. At **Mile 2.8**, you return to the hiking trail. There is an intersection just before **Mile 3**, where you ride straight across and then take a hard left. The trail climbs a hill and a lake to the south is visible in the late fall after the leaves drop or the early spring.

At **Mile 3.6**, the trail swings right and within a quarter mile

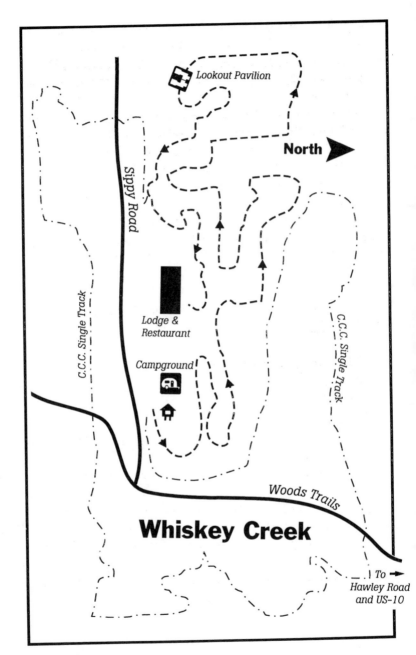

Lookout Pavilion

North

Sippy Road

C.C.C. Single Track

C.C.C. Single Track

Lodge & Restaurant

Campground

Woods Trails

Whiskey Creek

To Hawley Road and US-10

passes a dirt road on the right. Near **Mile 4** you take a left and climb a very steep hill for a third of a mile before racing down its backside. The trail swings left, climbs another hill and at **Mile 5** arrives at the lookout area. Perched on some of the highest hills along the route are large covered pavilions that make this spot ideal for an extended break. On a nice day in October, you can kick back for a spell and take in the fall colors.

From the lookout pavilions, the trail heads left in a northerly direction and eventually southeast towards the lodge. At **Mile 5.6**, you arrive at the back side of the lodge. Need a little more excercise? Take a right onto the single track just beyond the lodge for a half mile climb up a short, twisty hill. You end up descending into the camping area just a few hundred yards from the lodge for a 6.2 mile ride.

Please note that new trails and routes may be marked before and after race weekends, so mileages and distances may vary from time to time.

Heartland

A mountain biker double checks his rear derailleur on his tandem bicycle. The use of tandem bikes for off-road riding has increased noticeably in recent years.

Grand River County Park

County: Ingham
Total Mileage: 4.5 miles
Terrain: Generally flat with some gentle hills
Fees: Annual park pass or daily vehicle entry permit
Difficulty: Easy

Grand River Park was recently renamed William M. Burchfield Park and along with Riverbend Natural Area and McNamara Landing form a unique 540-acre system of county parks that not only welcomes mountain biking but encourages with rental bikes. All three parks border the Grand River and include second growth forest, reclaimed farmlands now turned to meadows and several impressive trees along the river itself.

The trails are relatively flat except for the Purple Loop, which features S-turns, soft climbs among the trees and descents. The rest of the system was built as hiking trails and are straight, easy rides. The trails are scenic, however, offering views of the river while traversing a mix of forests and open fields.

Trailheads are located at the north end of Grand River Park, Riverbend Natural Area and at McNamara Landing, the south end of the system. All trailheads have parking and are well posted. Water and restrooms are available at the Grand River entrance and along the trail.

Be aware that poison ivy is present but most of the trails are mowed, limiting your chances of encountering it. The loops and spurs are color coded and correspond to a trail guide brochure available at the contact stations. On the trail, the Blue and Red loops are the best marked.

Mountain bikes are available at this recreation area as hourly, half day or full day rental, and in combination with canoe rental. This makes the park an excellent destination for novice riders or families entering the sport.

When the ski season begins, generally late December, bikes are not allowed on the trails. The date you can begin biking also fluctuates from year to year due to spring flooding of the Grand River. It's always wise to call the park first if planning to ride in late spring or early summer.

Getting There: From I-96, just south of Lansing, depart at exit 101 and head south on M-99. Turn left on Waverly Road and then left onto Holt Road in a mile. The park is posted at the corner of Grovenburg Road. Head south on Grovenburg Road for 2 miles to the entrance of Grand River Park or 3 miles to Riverbend Natural Area at the west end of Nichols Road. McNamara Landing is reached by turning south onto Kingman Road from Nichols and west on Columbia Road.

Information: Contact Ingham County Parks, P.O. Box 38, Mason, MI 48854; ☎ (517) 676-2233. Recorded information is obtained by calling ☎ (517) 676-6109.

Grand River Trail
Distance: 4.5 miles
Trail: Single track
Direction: Clockwise
At Grand River Park the trailhead is located between two

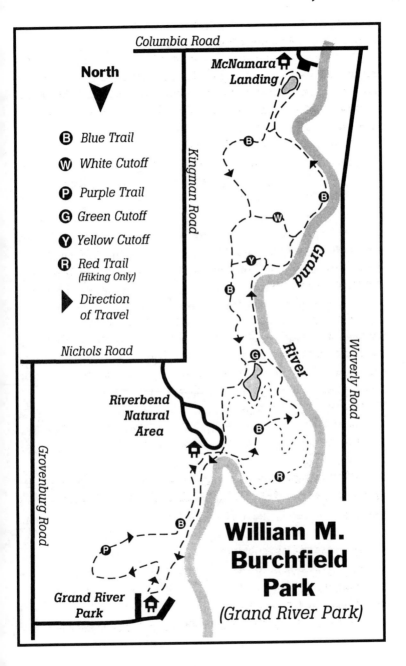

parking lots, which have signs directing you to it. Almost immediately is the Purple Loop (near the toboggan run) which is a single track and twists between the trees. There aren't any big hills along this loop but you encounter a few gentle slopes before the trail dips back into the woods and intersects the main trail, posted in red and blue.

Head left on the main trail as it descends a small hill and then gently climbs towards Grand River. The return loop is visible through the trees. The Riverbend Natural Area trailhead is reached in a half mile. Also located at the intersection a pair of vault toilets. The nearby Orange Loop is for cross county skiers only and not open to bikers.

The trail continues its gentle meandering, making it an easy stretch for people new to the feel of a mountain bike. This stretch doesn't require all of your attention, takes you casually through the Queen Ann's Lace and then moves you downhill into the woods where a bridge leads to the second intersection with the Red Loop.

The Blue Loop then skirts a meadow on one side and woods on the other and observant riders will see wild roses, black raspberries, dewberries, and native Monarda clustered here along in July. You move through a field bordered by 30-foot pines.

At **Mile 1.3** the Green cutoff appears and heads south past Meron Pond for the those who want to shorten their ride. The Blue Loop continues south through more meadows until you reach the Yellow cutoff at **Mile 1.8**. At this point you dip into the woods and cross a series of three bridges as the trail passes through the floodplains of the Grand River. This section can be wet or totally under the water in the spring. But later in the year it's dry and allows you to ride right to the banks of the Grand River.

You pass the last cutoff and then arrive at McNamara Landing, where there are vault toilets, parking and a boat landing for canoers. Head north and then east on the return route as the Blue Loop passes the last cutoff and then crosses old farm fields via mowed pathways. You pass the posted junctions of earlier crossover trails along with a few shady spots and a small bridge. The riding is easy in these rolling fields.

Just before **Mile 4**, the Blue Loop returns to the Riverbend trailhead and parking lot. This time head left on the loop marked in blue and red for a scenic stretch that skirts the high banks of the Grand River. A brief rise in the trail leads riders to the cabin and water pump before dipping down and passing a hiker's trail. At the end you return to the toboggan area and pass a picnic shelter before finally returning to the trailhead with its many intersecting paths.

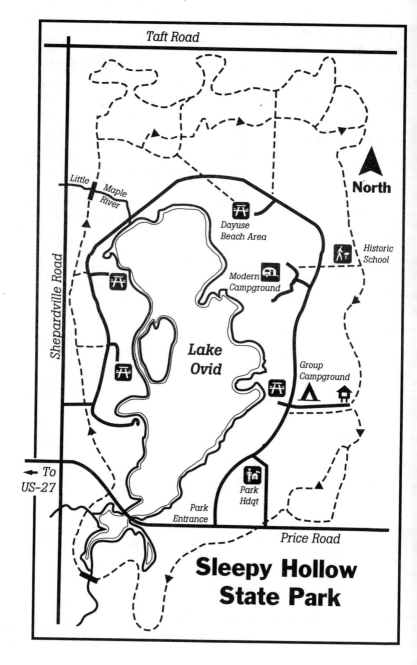

North

Sleepy Hollow State Park

Taft Road

Little
Maple
River

Shepardville Road

To US-27

Lake Ovid

Dayuse Beach Area

Modern Campground

Historic School

Group Campground

Park Entrance

Park Hdqt

Price Road

Sleepy Hollow State Park

County: Clinton
Total Mileage: 9 miles
Terrain: Reclaimed farmlands and woods.
Fees: Annual state park pass or daily vehicle entry permit.
Difficulty: Easy

Sleepy Hollow State Park is a lightly used 2,600-acre unit surrounding Lake Ovid just north of Lansing. The trail winds through wetlands, reclaimed farm fields and woods while crossing the Little Maple River twice. Much of it is flat terrain spiced with a few bits of elevation in the wooded areas.

Generally the southern parts of the trail system are mushy, particularly in spring when long stretches are submerged and spontaneous re-routing is required to negotiate the system. A small granny gear is advisable for early in the season since water on grass is like riding in peanut butter. The northern half has substantially less mud and more single track.

Due to numerous hunting access lots, trailheads abound. But to keep things simple, only the group campground trailhead is described here. To reach this trailhead, drive north

193

of the contact station and turn right at the second road for the group campground. Follow the dirt road to the trailhead at end. There are vault toilets at the trailhead, a water pump in the group campground and restrooms in the modern campground nearby.

Getting There: From Lansing head north on US-27 for 12 miles to Price Road. Turn east on Price to reach the park entrance in 6.5 miles.

Information: Contact the park headquarters at Sleepy Hollow State Park, 7835 Price Road, Laingsburg, MI 48848; ☎ (517) 651-6217.

Sleepy Hollow Loop

Distance: 9 miles
Trail: Single-track
Direction: Two way trail

At the trailhead you can head north or south where the trail rolls through damp woods that are covered with dog-tooth lilies as well as water in the spring! Riding at this time of the year is challenging, requiring a lot of stamina and bike handling to stay out of the mud and keep from getting soaked. The best season to ride this stretch is in the fall when the trail is relatively dry and very pleasant. In the autumn, the fields are filled with Joe Pye weed and clover to resemble old farmlands.

Within a quarter mile is the intersection for a loop that meanders through the woods. Stay right and at the next intersection keep to the left to avoid the link to the park manager's residence. Nearby is a posted intersection where the trail heads right through the low brush and out into open fields with Michigan lilies in late summer. Eventually you cross a ditch and Price Road near Upton Road. The next stretch is through a low marsh-like area that is often wet and sloppy in the spring. These fields end with a right turn and the welcome sight of a narrow, windy single track through the woods. This sweet piece of trail winds around stumps, rocks and roots along the lower edge of a ridge before climbing through beech and thornapple trees. At **Mile 2.6** a steep ravine cuts the ridge in half and rockets you up the opposite side.

You pass an overlook and descend into a field where Price Road and the southern end of Ovid Lake are visible on the right. Heading north, you cross the Little Maple River for the first time just beyond **Mile 3** via a dubious bridge. On the other side, turn right and follow the pond ignoring two hunter's access trails on the left, the second one passed at **Mile 3.6**.

Eventually the trail sends you rocketing into a ravine where at the bottom is a bridge that warrants controlled speed. Check this bridge out closely because usually it is not ridable. You climb out of the ravine into old farm fields and near **Mile 4** cross Price Road again. Pick up the trail at the post almost directly across the road. You pass through open fields that overlook the lake and then reach the fishing night entrance road at **Mile 4.6**. To the east this road leads to a dock on the lake where there is a small concession stand and vault toilets. Additional vault toilets are also at the next two trail junctions where short spurs lead east across the park road to picnic areas. The first picnic area is at **Mile 5** and is a nice spot to take an extended break.

The trail enters the woods beyond the picnic areas and at **Mile 6** crosses the Little Maple River for the second time. You then arrive at the first of many short loops scattered along the north part of the system. Make a jog right and then left a few hundred yards later to cross the hiking trail that leads south into the beach area.

Much of the northern end of the system is small hills and meadows with very little marsh. Several of the hills are interesting, including a sobering climb after you pass a loop intersection at **Mile 7.5**. The last intersection is reached within a quarter mile and from here you head south into a mix of small woodlots and old farm fields. A historic schoolhouse is reached at **Mile 8.4** where a spur heads west to the modern campground. From here the trailhead and the end of the 9-mile loop is reached in a little more than a half mile.

Taking on a short slope along the *Chief Cob-Moo-Sa Trail* in the Ionia Recreation Area east of Grand Rapids. The mountain bike area features a 9-mile system along the *Grand River.*

Ionia
Recreation Area

County: Ionia
Total Mileage: 9 miles
Terrain: Grand River, gravel pits and wooded ridges.
Fees: Annual state park pass or daily vehicle entry permit.
Difficulty: Moderate to strenuous

Ionia Recreation Area is a 4,018-acre state park unit in Ionia County, offering a wide range of outdoor activities that now includes mountain biking. Named after an Ottawa Indian chief who maintained a camp on the Grand River, most of the 9-mile Chief Cob-Moo-Sa Trail System is on the north side of Riverside Drive and is connected to the rest of the park by a two-track that begins in the Sessions Lake dayuse area.

The trail is mostly single track built in and around an abandoned gravel pit and railroad right-of-way. The surface is dirt and loose gravel with a few scattered patches of sand.

The main loop of the mountain biking trail is a technical challenge for most beginner and intermediate riders. Beginners can ride the system, but may need to walk many sections. Bikers will find a lot of tight turns and off-camber

short hills with many rocks and logs to hop over and around. For this reason a new 2.5-mile loop was built in 1996 that offers beginners a flat, level route.

The designated mountain biking trails are open year round but avoid the system during spring thaw or when trail is excessively wet and muddy. Stay off equestrian trails that crisscross the park as well as dog run areas and wildlife habitat areas. During the summer, Ionia Recreation Area maintains complete facilities, including modern restrooms, drinking water, camping, a beach area on Sessions Lake and concession stands.

Getting There: Ionia is located off I-96 between Grand Rapids and Lansing. Depart at exit 64 and head north on Jordan Lake Road. Within 3 miles the park entrance is reached. From the park office you can obtain a map that will direct you to various parking locations near the trailhead.

Information: Contact Ionia Recreation Area, 2880 West David Hwy, Ionia, MI 48846; ☎ (616) 527-3750 or call the MMBA ☎ (616) 785-0120.

Chief Cob-Moo-Sa Trail

Distance: 7.2 miles from Sessions Lake
Trail: Single track
Direction: Counter clockwise

Starting from the main park area at the Sessions Lake beach, you ride north for 0.7 miles to Riverside Drive and the main loop. It's a two-track downhill that is intersected by an equestrian trail - so ride with care. There is a unique marsh area on the west side of the two-track and on any given day you may see egrets, great blue herons, a variety of ducks, hawks and other wildlife. It pays to ride this section of the trail slowly and enjoy the scenery. Once you enter the main trail loop, you may not have the opportunity to take your eyes off the trail as much.

The two track ends at Riverside Drive with the historical Ionia Sheriff's Posse House directly across the road. The trail heads east through a field in front of the fenced-in building and ends at the Riverside Parking and Picnic area in less than a mile. This

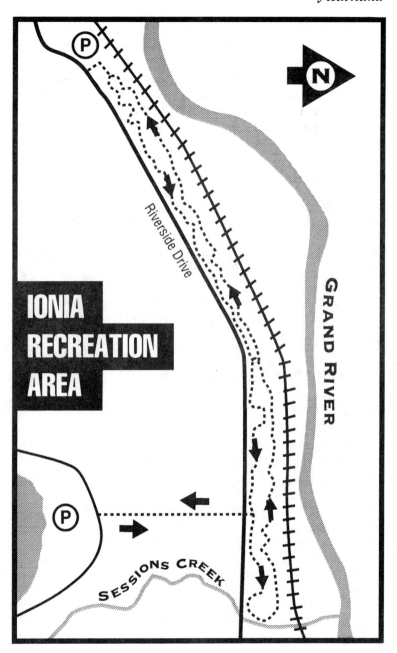

IONIA RECREATION AREA

Riverside Drive

GRAND RIVER

SESSIONS CREEK

Mountain bikers cross an open field towards a gravel pit area in the Ionia Recreation Area.

parking area is an optional staging site for bikers.

From the north end of the parking area, the trail continues east and begins by skirting a low ridge and then makes a short descent to Sessions Creek. You stay with the creek briefly and pass a railroad trestle before swinging west and at **Mile 2.4** reach a dirt access road to a boat launch on the Grand River.

The trail continues west across the road. Here the trail becomes a very interesting ride as it skirts a ridge that runs parallel to the railroad tracks below. This portion of the trail has a lot of off-camber sections with roots and rocks and twisting turns up and around various parts of the ridge. On wet days or if your bike tires are not up to trail riding standards, the off-camber trail can be a real challenge. At **Mile 3.7**, 2 miles from the Riverside parking lot, you come to an "Y" intersection. The fork to the south-east is a crossover spur for those who only want to ride 3 miles.

Just beyond the spur, you break out at an overgrown gravel pit where the trail finally levels out. Just when you start to relax with the easy riding, a caution signs pops up and the trail races back down the riverside bluff along a series of tight switchbacks. At this point the trail remains along the railroad tracks with the bluffs rising on one side of you and views of the Grand River through the trees on the other side.

At **Mile 4.7**, the trail splits off in two directions again. The fork to the west (left) quickly reaches a dirt road which you can follow to return to Riverside Drive or a second boat launch on the Grand River. Plans call for this spot to be developed as a future staging area and parking lot.

The main trail is posted and swings east to a stretch of short, steep climbs through a series of old gravel pits along with rocks, gravel and a little bit of sand. Down by the river you were squeezing through the trees; in this stretch you weave around large boulders. At **Mile 5.7** you skirt the largest pit and at one point you're on the edge looking nervously down at a 30-foot drop. From the pit, the trail parallels Riverside Drive on one side and a large marshy area on the other before shooting back into the woods to intersect the crossover spur.

Your front shocks, tires and even eyeballs will be thoroughly tested as the entire trail is full of dirt mounds, roots, rocks and gravel runouts and weaves back and forth more times than you care to count. At **Mile 6.7** you end up back at the Sheriff's Posse House on Riverside Drive and the end of the loop.

You can ride back to the Sessions Lake beach area for a total trip of 7.2 miles and in the summer hit the water to cool down. The trail is also within riding distance of the town of Ionia, a 4-mile trip, via Riverside Drive, where you'll find restaurants and other shops.

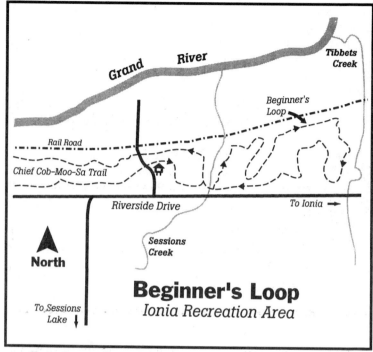

Beginner's Loop
Ionia Recreation Area

Beginner's Loop

Distance: 2.5 miles
Trail: Single track
Direction: Clockwise

The beginner's loop is picked up at the Riverside Drive dayuse area, where you begin by following the main trail east at the north end of the parking lot. You skirt a low bluff briefly and then make a short descent to Sessions Creek. But instead of paralleling the creek north along the main route, the new loop crosses it on Riverside Drive.

On the other side you follow the loop in a clockwise direction as it winds through the brush and a sapling forest. Halfway through the loop, you swing close to Tibbets Creek before the trail swings west for the return. After recrossing Sessions Creek, you follow the main trail until it crosses the dirt road to the Grand River boat launch. Head south on the dirt road to quickly arrive at the dayuse area.

Cannonsburg Ski Area

County: Kent
Total Mileage: 3 miles
Terrain: Wooded hills and open ski hills
Fees: None
Difficulty: Easy

Cannonsburg Ski Area appeals to bikers who like climbing hills and getting momentarily lost - yeah, you read that right. The bright side, however, is the steep slopes and the solitude that can be enjoyed. If you're into climbing hills for training or building endurance, Cannonsburg can be enjoyed even if you're not familiar with the unmarked trails.

The course is spread out over a few hundred acres of woods and the open ski hills, providing a unique riding opportunity in the Grand Rapids area. The hills have a vertical rise of close to 300 feet while some of the slopes are more than a quarter mile in length. The grass is cut throughout the summer so you can climb the slopes if your legs and technical skills can handle it. There is a pleasant view from the top of the ski hills even though you're just minutes away from Grand

Rapids.

It is important to remember that the Cannonsburg Ski Area is privately-held land. Presently the managers don't charge a trail fee, but ask that you do not stray onto private property adjacent to the ski area.

There are no facilities on site in the summer, but bathrooms with drinking water are open at the softball fields near the entrance to the ski lodge when teams are playing. You can ride from the end of ski season until Nov. 15. If snow flies early or late, riding is suspended in lieu of skiing activities. The trails are also closed for symphony concert dates when a temporary pavilion and seats are set up on ski hills in July. And finally, night riding is prohibited.

The Cannonsburg Ski Area stages two mountain biking races annually in the spring and fall. During these events, the ski area is openly to only registered racers.

Getting There: Cannonsburg is 15 miles northeast of Grand Rapids. From I-96 in Grand Rapids, depart at exit 38 and head north on East Belt Line (M-44). After crossing the Grand River, turn east on Cannonsburg Road and in 6 miles the ski area will be on the south side.

Information: Contact the Cannonsburg Ski Area, 6800 Cannonsburg Rd., Cannonsburg, MI 439317; ☎ (616) 874-6711.

Cannonsburg Ski Area

Distance: 3 miles
Track: Single and two-track
Direction: None

Parking is next to the lodge, where three bridges cross the creek to the bottom of the ski hills. The trails are not signed and there are many crisscrossing routes. Most of the riding is done in the woods where there are some sandy sections. If you head east

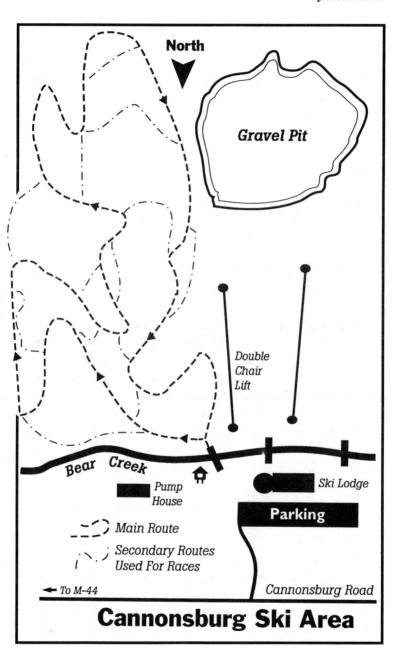

North

Gravel Pit

Double
Chair
Lift

Bear Creek

Pump
House

Ski Lodge

Parking

Main Route

Secondary Routes
Used For Races

To M-44

Cannonsburg Road

Cannonsburg Ski Area

from the bottom of the double chair lift and ride in a clockwise direction, you'll find the loose, sandy segments of the trail are approached going downhill.

This will make the ride more enjoyable and the sand less predominant. During the spring and fall, there is good visibility through the sparse foliage and you will be rewarded with views of the ski hills as well as the terrain that surrounds the ski area.

The length of the ride is 2 to 3 miles depending on which trails you follow. Keep in mind that on the southwest side of the ski hills is a gravel and sand pit. If you are exploring the trails, the pit will be the western boundary of your ride, the creek the northern boundary and private land will form the boundary to the east and south.

The best way to follow these trails is to ride them prior to one of the two race events held here. The race route is marked a week before for practice and, of course, for the race itself. At that time, you can follow the temporary directional signs and gradually learn some of the possible combinations and loops that have been laid out.

You can also combine the 7-mile ride at Cannonsburg State Game Area with the Cannonsburg Ski Area for 15-mile day. The best route from one area to the other is to follow Cannonsburg Road to Egypt Valley Road and then to Four Mile Road, a 2-mile ride each way.

On such an outing during the summer the Cannonsburg Game Area is often as crowded as ants on a sugar cube while the ski area, because of its limited trail system, will have only one or two cars in the parking lot.

Cannonsburg State Game Area

County: Kent
Total Mileage: 7.2 miles
Terrain: Forested hills, some two-tracks
Fees: None
Difficulty: Easy to moderate

The state game areas are the latest division of the Michigan Department of Natural Resources to incorporate a limited concept of "recreation" into their management plans. Traditionally, the sole focus of game areas was hunting, fishing and some limited forest management practices. But now DNR managers of this diverse group of public land has recognized other forest users including, in some cases, mountain bikers.

Still the primary focus of state game area management is hunting and fishing due to the formula by which these areas receive their state and federal money. In short, license fees from hunters and anglers make the purchase of most game areas possible.

The 1,331-acre Cannonsburg State Game Area is a popular destination for many bikers in the Grand Rapids, thanks to a terrain that is surprisingly fun and interesting. The trail is mostly winding single track in a relatively flat

area. But due to the heavy use Cannonsburg gets, the trail can get fairly tricky as rock and roots become exposed and surface conditions change almost as frequently as the weather in Michigan.

One main loop crosses several dirt roads and uses a few short sections of two-tracks to skirt private land holdings within the game area. The large number of private lands give Cannonsburg its patchwork appearance. *It is extremely important to stay on the proper trails or avoid trespassing and fines.*

Beginners can easily handle this route while more experienced riders will find it a lot of fun when ridden at "speed." Always ride expecting to see other riders and trail users and be prepared to stop and yield on the trail.

Riding is March 1 to September 15th only. There is no riding in the winter because the trail is part of a much larger cross-country ski loop in Kent County. There is no night riding either.

Getting There: From I-96 in Grand Rapids, depart at exit 38 and head north on East Belt Line (M-44). After crossing the Grand River, turn east on Cannonsburg Road and then in 5 miles turn south on Egypt Valley Road. Turn east on Four Mile Road for a half mile to the bottom of a gravel hill. The parking lot is on the south side of Four Mile Road and the trailhead is on the north side.

Information: Contact the Flat River State Game Area, 6640 Long Lake Rd., Belding, MI 48809; ☎ (616) 794-2658. The route is maintained by the Western Michigan Chapter of the Michigan Mountain Biking Association. For trail maintenance dates call the chapter at ☎ (616) 785-0120.

Cannonsburg State Game Area

Distance: 7.2 miles
Trail: Single track with some two-track roads.
Direction: Clockwise suggested
Although the trail is not extensively marked, it's used enough

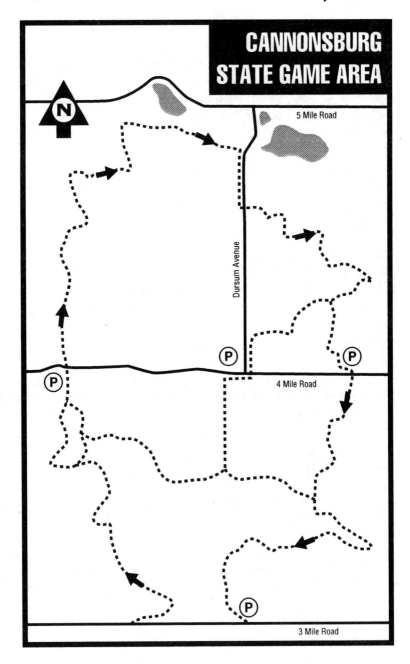

CANNONSBURG STATE GAME AREA

5 Mile Road

Dursum Avenue

4 Mile Road

3 Mile Road

so getting lost would be difficult. From the parking lot head north across Four Mile Road and follow the trail through rolling terrain where you may encounter some sand and mud. At **Mile 1.5**, you reach a "Y" intersection. Continuing on the loop requires a sharp right here to head southeast onto another section of the game area. You can bail out of the loop by continuing north at the intersection to reach Five Mile Road, where its possible to return to the parking lot via the roads. Heading southeast on the trail, you reach Dursum Road, a wide two-track, within a mile. Continue south (right) on Dursum for a couple of hundred yards and then re-enter the single track to the east (left).

Dursum Road runs into Four Mile Road, where to the west on Four Mile is the parking lot. But the trail heads southeast from Dursum Road into the prettiest and most technical segments of the route. The single track here features both short and steep hills and long, winding climbs. This is also where the most mud will be encountered, a good reason to stay off this section in the early spring. At **Mile 4.5** you emerge at Four Mile Road and again can return to the parking lot by heading west.

To continue on the trail, head east (left) on Four Mile Road for a few hundred yards and then pick up the single track on the south side of the road. *Be very alert for cars on Four Mile Road!* This is a hilly section of the road and motorists are not expecting to see a biker coming out of the woods.

Heading south again you climb some small hills and come to another "Y" intersection. Turn left and follow the trail as it crosses Egypt Creek, climbs several long hills and ends in a small parking lot on Three Mile Road at **Mile 5.7**. This is another possible staging area to park and begin the ride. Head west on the gravel road for a quarter mile and pick up the single-track on the north side of the road at the bottom of the small hill.

This last section of the trail is 1.5 miles long and crosses three bridges. After the third bridge you are only about a quarter mile from the parking lot on Four Mile Road where you began. Be careful around the bridges, some bikers believe trolls live under them and will grab your tire when your not looking!

Maple River State Game Area

County: Gratiot
Total Mileage: 8 miles
Terrain: Flat, open marshes and some woods
Fees: None
Difficulty: Easy

The Maple River State Game Area is a flood plain that straddles US-27 north of St. John's and during the right time of year can provide bikers with a scenic and easy ride. The 2,737-acre area is divided into two sections with the West Unit containing most of the acreage but no established trails other than a short access trails for handicapped hunters

Most of the riding is done in the East Unit, whose pools and diked-in ponds serve as the water basin for the Maple River. This makes the unit a stopover for migrating birds, including herons, Canada geese and a variety of waterfowl. The spectacular congregations of birds among the cattails in the warm glows of a late afternoon sun makes this limited trail system scenic and interesting, especially for families and those new to mountain biking.

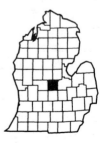

On the west side of US-27, you begin at a boat launch located at Croswell and Taft roads. The eastern trailhead is a parking area reached immediately after US-27 crosses to the north side of the flood plain. Both areas are open to hunting and bright colors or even blaze orange should be worn during the fall, especially during the October duck season.

Getting There: From St. John's, head north on US-27 for 8.5 miles. The eastern trailhead is a gated two-track in a parking lot off US-27 on the north side of the floodplains.

The shorter trail on the west side is reached by continuing north and then turning west (left) on Ranger Road. Within a mile turn south (left) on Croswell Road to its intersection with Taft Road. Avoid Taft and continue south on the dirt access road to the boat launch and parking area. The gate at the causeway is the trailhead.

Information: Contact the Rose Lake Research Center, 8562 East Stoll Rd, East Lansing, MI 48823; ☎ (517) 373-9358

West Unit

Distance: 2.3 miles round trip
Trail: Two-track on raised causeway
Direction: Two way

From the trailhead, the route is an arrow straight ride on a roadbed of pea gravel that within a quarter mile turns into grassy two-track. Here you'll find the trail a bit lumpy in the grass, which has a tendency to draw you into the ruts of the two-track.

You can't beat the scenery, however. This is a beautiful environment for bicycling as you pass between a quiet marsh on the left and a river channel on the right where it's possible at times to see a multitude of wildlife including waterfowl, turtles and mammals like muskrats and beavers.

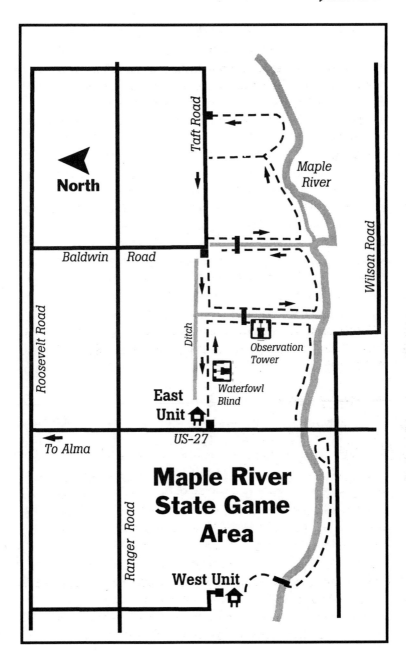

North

Taft Road

Maple River

Wilson Road

Baldwin Road

Roosevelt Road

Ditch

Observation Tower

Waterfowl Blind

East Unit

US-27

To Alma

Maple River State Game Area

Ranger Road

West Unit

With a little less than a mile left, the track swings from a southern to eastern direction and finally butts up to the embankment of US-27, where it's necessary to backtrack to return to the parking lot. Don't be fooled by the close proximity of the highway; this trail is a reward.

East Unit

Distance: 5.8 miles
Trail: Two-track on dikes
Direction: Two way

This ride is between two parking areas/boat launches in the East Unit and requires backtracking along much of the same route in order to return to your car. There are no facilities or drinking water at either the trailhead on US-27 or Taft Road.

Begin at the far end of the US-27 parking lot where there is a gate. From here a two-track of crushed slag heads east along a dike and within a half mile reaches a long boardwalk that extends into the cattails. At the other end is a barrier-free blind, a three-sided shelter that keeps hunters comfortable during the fall and camera lens dry the rest of the year. There is open water south of the blind, providing a biker the opportunity to quietly watch great blue herons, bitterns or other birds fishing.

Hopping back on the bike and continuing east, you cross a bridge and at **Mile 1** reach an observation tower, raising 20 feet above the marsh to provide a different vantage point of the winged wildlife. At the tower is bridge that leads to the opposite side of the canal, where you have a choice of heading left or right.

The right-hand fork leads around the southern edge of the game area and into a stands of trees that allows you to watch herons feed undisturbed. The trail here also skirts a wide section of the river and then jogs north to cross another canal via a second bridge. At this point you head south into stand of woods and then north arriving at Taft Road.

Turn left on Taft and then ride west to reach the second parking area that also provides access to the raised dike

The Maple River State Game Area features both wooded trails and open riding along dikes.

trails in the state game area. From this parking lot you backtrack along the same trails by first heading south and then west along the river. The final leg is to head north along the canal to the bridge across from the observation tower, where you are only a mile from the US-27 parking area and boat launch.

Bikers emerge from a segment of single track within Ithaca Jailhouse Trails. The mountain bike area is located at the Gratiot County Fairgrounds and does feature an old jailhouse along the course.

Ithaca Jailhouse Trails

County: Gratiot
Total Mileage: 3.3 miles
Terrain: Generally flat area of dense secondary growth and fields
Fees: None
Difficulty: Easy to moderate

Located next to the Gratiot County Fairgrounds, Ithaca Jailhouse Trails is a 52-acre patch of woods that 20 years ago was slated to become a historical park. A one-room school and a jailhouse were even relocated to the area before the plans fell apart.

In 1993, the city of Ithaca decided to turn the area into a mountain bike trail system and with the help of the MMBA un-veiled its course the following year. The name was a natural. Not only is there a jailhouse on site, but prisoners from the Mid-Michigan Correction Facility did most of the work.

Presently there is a 3.3-mile network that begins from a trailhead just off the fairground's entrance road. The main route is Jailhouse Trail, a 1.75-mile two track that winds pass small marshes, the jail and the only hill in the area of

any contour. There are four more single tracks that pass through woods or skirt open fields and nearly connect to make a separate loop of their own.

Despite a lack of hills or mileage, the designers have still created an interesting system by including a series of tight turns. The single tracks are considered moderately difficult rides, the two-track is easy, ideal for beginners and intermediate cyclists. The many lowlying areas have bridges and fill but can still be wet in the spring and damp throughout much the summer.

Camping is permitted at the fairgrounds, which includes a heated restroom and a picnic shelter.

Getting There: Depart US-27 on Business Loop US-27 and follow it as it becomes Center Street in downtown Ithaca. From Center turn south on Pine River Street and in 2 miles you reach the fairgrounds. Follow the entrance road of the fairgrounds as it heads left to the trailheads near an old red schoolhouse.

Information: Contact City of Ithaca, 129 West Emerson St, Ithaca, MI 48847; ☎ (517) 875-3200. Or call Terry's Cycle and Sports at ☎ (517) 463-5260.

Jailhouse Trails

Distance: 3 miles
Trail: Single track and some two-track
Direction: Two way

The two trailheads are north of the red schoolhouse, one nearby, the other posted closer to the fairgrounds. The easiest way to follow this track is to begin at the posted trailhead and ride in a counter-clockwise direction. This description uses the counter-clockwise route and begins by riding the two-track towards the schoolhouse and veering right before passing it.

The trail becomes single track shortly and heads into the dense swale that is typical for most of the ride. This first section in the woods is made interesting by the scattering of roots and

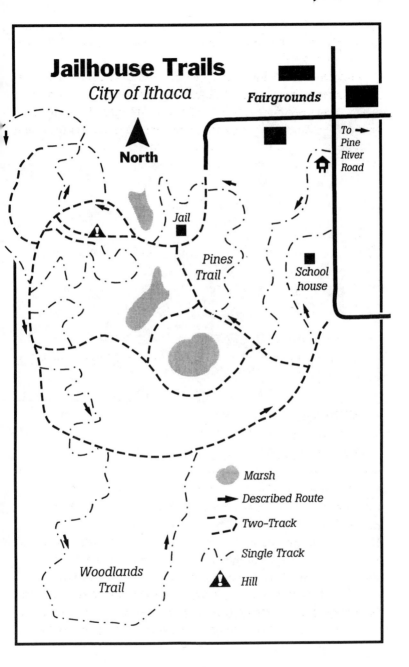

Heartland

Jailhouse Trails

City of Ithaca

North

Fairgrounds

To Pine River Road

Jail

Pines Trail

School house

Marsh

Described Route

Two-Track

Single Track

Hill

Woodlands Trail

A mountain biker adjusts his son's helmet before a race at Ithaca Jailhouse Trails. The Gratiot County biking area is the site of a race that attracts hundreds of bikers annually.

small stumps, especially early into the ride on a short descent into a ravine.

There are only a couple logs on this trail and the first one is reached within a half mile. This is closely followed by a technically challenging stretch that includes a right turn between two trees and large rocks that aren't quite a tire's width apart. The third part of this natural little wonder is a prominent root on the other side of the trees. Descending this is easier than ascending it.

At **Mile 1** are a pair of bridges as the track cuts through a lowlying area. This is not a good route for right after the spring thaw. Up to this point the ride has been in the shade of many wild apple, cherry and hawthorn trees, the reason many bikers carried extra spare tubes and race registration kits have included patch kits.

At **Mile 1.7** there is a sneaky little hill climb that is fun because of the off camber wind to the top. Another short and steep climb is reached just before **Mile 2**, where the trail ascends a ridge and then heads down the other side down on the only gravity sponsored free ride.

Within a third of a mile you reach a series of bridges through the woods that cries out *SPRING MUDFEST!* At **Mile 2.7** the trail pops out of the trees to the right onto a service road. After several yards the trail pops back into the woods before coming out onto the two-track one last time. You turn left with the two-track and head back to the parking lot.

Several laps alternating clockwise and counter-clockwise is a good way to keep the trail interesting and build the mileage up.

Mountain bikers walk their bikes across a swing bridge over the Chippewa River to reach the beginning of the Wildwood Pathway in Deerfield County Park, just west of Mount Pleasant.

Deerfield County Park

County: Isabella
Total Mileage: 8 miles
Terrain: Hardwood forests and river bluffs
Fees: Daily vehicle entry fee
Difficulty: Easy

Deerfield County Park is the largest public park in Isabella County at almost 600 acres and is split in the middle by the Chippewa River. This picturesque river not only gives the park its scenic qualities but also isolates the 8-mile trail system from the busy beach and picnic areas on the other side. As soon as you cross the river, via a suspension foot bridge, you enter a quiet backcountry area where it's possible to spot such wildlife as deer, wild turkeys and ruffled grouse.

The unqiue aspect of the park is Fisher Covered Bridge. This unusual bridge is such an endearing aspect of Deerfield that it was quickly rebuilt in 1996 after it mysteriously caught fire the year before. The structure is the only covered bridge in Michigan that is on a mountain bike trail.

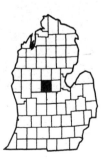

Along with the bridge, the river and the wildlife, Deerfield also features an 8-mile trail system, shared in the summer by mountain bikers and hikers, and groomed in the winter for cross country skiers. The heart of the system is the 2.8-mile Wildwood Pathway, which was designated as a National Recreation Trail in 1980 by the U.S. Department of Interior because of its forested beauty.

The most scenic trail in the park, however, is the River Loop and together they can be combined for a 5.7-mile ride where you retrace only one leg of Wildwood Pathway. The system also has numerous crossover spurs and side trails, allowing riders a variety of routes to choose from.

Facilities within the park include a swimming area, shelter and picnic area, water and vault toilets. Along the trail there are two water pumps and a backcountry campground for canoers and hikers.

Keep in mind that the area is heavily used by hikers, who always have right-of-way on trails. Biking is also prohibited when there are three inches or more of snow or more on the ground. Like cross country skiers, bikers should also follow the trail system counter clockwise.

Getting There: From US-27, depart at Mount Pleasant and follow M-20 west for 6.5 miles. The entrance is on M-20 and inside the park there is separate parking for the Wildwood Pathway trailhead.

Information: Contact the Isabella County Parks and Recreation Commission, 200 North Main St., Mount Pleasant, MI 48858; ☎ (517) 772-0911.

Wildwood Pathway and River Loop

Distance: 5.7 miles
Trail: Single track
Direction: Counter clockwise

The most techincal aspect of the entire ride is reached within minutes after you have locked up the car. From the trailhead, it's less than a 100 yards to a very narrow and bouncy suspension

The Deerfield County Park trail system includes the only covered bridge along a mountain biking route in Michigan. Fisher Covered Bridge crosses the Chippewa River and is used to reach a short piece of trail on the west side of the river.

bridge over the Chippewa River. *You must carry your bike across* and that's still no easy task. But this bridge serves as a passage into the park's backcountry, which, thanks to the Chippewa River, is a world away from the busy beach and picnic areas on the other side.

From the bridge you head south on Wildwood Pathway but quickly turn right onto River Loop. The trail begins as a wood-chip path and swings past a bend in the Chippewa and then gently climbs the riverside bluffs for the first of the many scenic views.

Within a half mile is the posted junction to Fisher Covered Bridge. First built in 1968 then rebuilt in 1996, today the covered bridge is the only one in Michigan's that is reached soley by foot, bicycle or ski. On the other side of the bridge is the mile-long

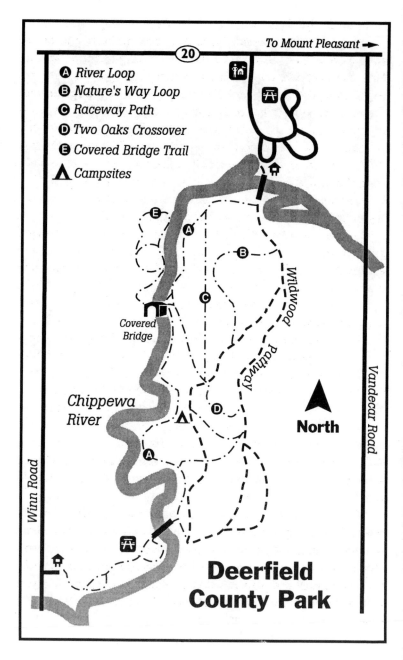

Covered Bridge Trail around an old walleye rearing pond.

You skirt more riverside bluffs after the junction to the bridge and, just beyond **Mile 1**, pass a short spur to Wildwood Pathway. Near the junction is the park's backcountry campground with sites overlooking the Chippewa River, making them very popular with canoeists on a overnight paddle. Within the campground is a water pump. River Loop resumes skirting the bluffs and then at **Mile 1.5** passes a spur to a second suspension bridge. This bridge crosses the Chippewa to a picnic area with tables but no water. Just beyond the bridge the River Loop joins Wildwood Pathway.

Continue on the pathway in a counter clockwise direction. You pass through a scenic wooded stretch and then come to a split in the trail with a "Steep Hill!" sign posted on the right-hand fork. Up to this point the trail has been exceptionally level and easy with the only varation being the short climbs up the river bluffs. But on the Steep Hill spur, you struggle to the top of a hill and then rocket down a 40-foot slope that bottoms out at a soft patch of dirt where the trail takes 90-degree turn.

The other fork is a bypass for this hill and the two merge together at **Mile 2**, just before the junction with Fire Break Crossover, one of three crossover spurs within Wildwood Pathway. Follw any of them for a little more variation in elevation.

Wildwood Pathway continues north, passes Two Oaks Crossover in a quarter mile and then enters a stretch of forest that is often muddy and wet during the summer. At **Mile 2.75**, you reach the two-way segment of Wildwood Pathway. If you head north at this point, the trailhead is a quarter of a mile away.

To lengthen the ride, head south for another loop through the park. This leg of Wildwood Pathway is 1.2 miles long and for the most part is a wide and level trail through the woods until you reach the southern end of the loop. Here you head north along the segment of the pathway already experienced, providing you with another opportunity for a downhill ride on the Steep Hill spur.

Brian Cool at the main lodge of Cool's Cross Country Farm. The resort features a trail system for cross country skiing and mountain biking and hosts bikes races annually.

Cool's Cross Country Farm

County: Osceola
Total Mileage: 25 miles
Terrain: Woods, rolling hills and open fields
Fees: Trail pass
Difficulty: Easy to moderate

Cool's Cross Country Farm is like going to your grandfather's farm and exploring the back 40 acres on your mountain bike. Operated by Brian Cool and his family, the center is a hilly tract of woods, open fields, two lakes and a handful of old barns and cabins. Winding through this farm is a 25-mile trail system made up of mostly two-tracks and forest roads that can be combined for any type of ride you're looking for; short and sweet for beginners to long and challenging for more advanced riders.

A favorite of cross country skiers since 1976, the center has been discovered by a growing number of mountain bikers in recent years. You'd need a day, or even two, to explore all the possible route combinations. Or arrive during the annual Mike Cool Memorial Challenge, an event staged in memory of Brian's father.

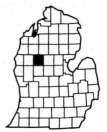

Calling the Memorial Challenge a race, however, is a bit of a misnomer. Except for the top ten riders, it is more like a tour and a great way

229

to get to know the area. The race day course varies from 10 to 14 miles in length and is set up as a continuous loop through the best terrain for mountain bikes.

Facilities at the center include a lakeshore campground, rustic cabins and bunkhouse accommodations. There is also a restaurant in the lodge that serves good breakfasts and the best chili on the west side of the state. Cool's Cross Country Farm is open to mountain biking from April 1 until they begin grooming the trails for skiers, generally in mid-December. Keep in mind that both Cool's Farm and the surrounding land is used heavily during the firearm deer season (Nov. 15-30).

During less busy times, payment for the use of the mountain bike trails is on the honor system with a deposit box at the entrance to the parking lot. Many times you'll have the place to yourself. When that happens, be grateful for the solitude. This is when Cool's Cross Country Farm is the "coolest" place to ride.

Getting There: Cool's Cross Country Farm is 60 miles north of Grand Rapids. From US-131 depart at exit 162 and head west and then north on 210th Avenue immediately after crossing the highway. Within 2.5 miles 210th Avenue crosses LeRoy Road and then passes the entrance to Cool's.

Information: Contact Cool Ski Area, 5557 N. 210th Ave. LeRoy, MI 49655; ☎ (616) 768-4624.

Cool's Cross Country Farm
Distance: 4.5 miles
Trail: Two-tracks and forest roads
Direction: None

In 1996, the trail signs at Cool's were changed and upgraded and a new map was produced. Still this can be a confusing trail system to follow due to many junctions that are not posted and many trails and two-tracks not shown on the map. This can be fun if you're looking for an adventure in the woods or frustrating if you always like to know where you are.

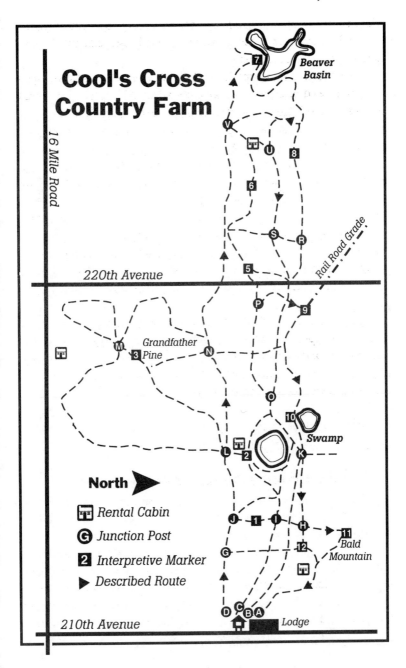

Cool's Cross Country Farm

Beaver Basin

16 Mile Road

220th Avenue

Grandfather Pine

Rail Road Grade

Swamp

North

Rental Cabin

G Junction Post

2 Interpretive Marker

Described Route

Bald Mountain

Lodge

210th Avenue

This route was chosen because it is scenic and easy to follow. Most of the route is "easy" in difficulty because there are no twisty single track sections that require technical skills. However, you will encounter both sand and occasional wet marsh-like areas along the trail.

From behind the lodge, head south towards the D Trail, which begins by passing through a gate. You then follow a mowed path through a farm field and descend to Post G reached within a quarter mile of the lodge. Continue straight, but be careful as the trail descends towards a low lying wet area in the woods then immediately climbs out to Post J.

Post J is a confusing junction. Turn right on the most northerly trail which immediately descends a hill and bottoms out at Interpretive Marker 1. A set of numbered markers have been erected along the system as a self-guiding nature trail. The first one marks a stand of hemlock. You climb out of the ravine and at **Mile 0.5** reach Post I at what appears to be a forest road.

This is the service trail used to take guests and supplies to the cabins scattered throughout the tract. Turn left (west) and follow it until you come within view of Lake Arthur. At this point leave the service trail and turn left (south) on a trail. You'll skirt the small lake, come within view of the campground on the opposite shore, pass a rental cabin and come to Post L at **Mile 0.8**.

Post L is another major junction. Two trails depart south from here towards Grandfather Pine at Interpretive Marker 3. This 40-foot white pine is an impressive sight, but the trails in this section of the farm are poorly marked and can be difficult to follow.

The third trail at Post L heads straight or due west and quickly connects into an old dirt road. Near **Mile 1** is Post N, where the trails from the Grandfather Pine re-connect to the main system. Continue heading west. You'll endure some sandy sections, pass a few trails not on the map and then at **Mile 1.4** arrive at 220th Avenue, a graded dirt road.

On the other side of the road the trail continues heading west towards Beaver Basin. You pass a few more trails, come within sight of a rental cabin and at **Mile 1.8** reach Post V. Take the trail to the far left for a delightful run through the hilly woods. The two-track ends at Interpretive Marker 7, site of a huge beaver pond reached at **Mile 2.2**. To see the dam you must head left and cross a small bridge to the west side of the pond. It's better to walk this portion than to ride your bike.

Back at Interpretive Marker 7, head right (east) to continue the loop. There are several overgrown two-tracks in this area, but the main trail is easy to recognize and follow. It swings to the north and leads you through an open meadow before heading east. Eventually you descend a ridgeline of pines and then emerge at Post U at **Mile 2.7**. From this junction you can see a picturesque cabin to the south. The service road departs due east while heading northeast is a two-track through a pine plantation that passes Post S and then returns to 220th Avenue at **Mile 3**.

On the other side of the dirt road is another junction. Head left (north) on the trail marked by blue blazes for one of the best segments of trail at the Cool's Farm. You begin with a mild climb and then follow an old railroad grade through the woods. At **Mile 3.3** the blue blazes lead you away from the railroad grade to an open field where you ride above a scenic swamp area, passing Interpretive Marker 10 along the way.

After skirting the swamp, a junction of three trails (Post K on the map) is reached. By choosing the two-track in the middle, you will quickly arrive at Post H and the main spur to Bald Mountain. Turn left and at **Mile 4** you will reach this "peak", the highest point on the trail system. At 1,525 feet, Bald Mountain is only 200 feet less than the highest point in the Lower Peninsula - Grove Hill just to the east. You break out in a sweat climbing to the top of the grassy knoll, where Interpretive Marker 11 is planted, but the view is nice and the run down its backside fun.

You shoot down its east side along a mowed strip in a field and then climb another hill from which you can view a red barn to the north. Eventually the trail heads into the woods where another rental cabin is located. There are many trails in this area, but by keeping a southeast course, you quickly pass other cabins and reach the main lodge and restaurant at the trailhead.

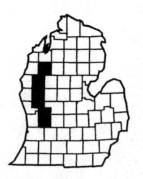

North County
Trail

Within the Huron-Manistee National Forest, a portion of the North Country Trail is open to Mountain Bikers and a portion is designated for foot travel only.

Mountain Biking On The NCT

In 1996, the U.S. Forest Service (USFS), which administers the Huron-Manistee National Forests, completed a long awaited study of the North Country Trail (NCT) and the results of it are straight forward and easy to understand:

Roughly 80 miles are open to mountain bikers, 30 miles are closed. Of course, the entire trail is open to hiking.

The study emerged from five different scenarios that were proposed for the management of this section of the North Country Trail. They ranged from completely opening the NCT to mountain biking to completely closing it.

Some National Park Service officials, who administer the trail on a national level, were opposed to bikes on any section of it. Many USFS officials welcomed a non-motorized multi-use policy while the NCT membership was somewhat divided. Members of the Michigan Mountain Biking Association, meanwhile, were helping to maintain the trail in their effort to continue to use it.

Basically, every group which had been using the trail for the past several years was waiting for an official position from the USFS, to see where they fit in. And it finally came.

Many users, one trail, it's not hard to understand the controversy that surrounded the NCT. The biggest complaint from hikers was the lost of solitude when bikers zipped past them. It was that expectation of trekking alone for miles that beckoned them to shoulder a pack in hopes of discovering a wilderness-like solitude and the freedom that comes with it. For mountain bikers, the adventure of meeting Mother Nature through the eyes of dynamic motion has always lured out the child within us. In riding a bike, there is a always a child-like joy and, as R.L. Stevenson, put it "to miss the joy is to miss it all."

But the debate is over and the sharing has begun. Our care and responsibility for the trail is now duty. As mountain bikers we must share the sections open to us and abstain from riding on those sections closed to multi-use. The closed sections are from Dilling Road South to M-55 (10 miles); from the Bowman Lake trailhead near Baldwin south to Nichols Lake (17 miles); and from M-20 south to Croton Dam (19 miles). Still mountain bikers can enjoy some of the NCT's most glorious and inspiring segments, including from the Marilla trailhead south to Dilling Road and from US-10 north through Freesoil.

This is not to say that the pine plantations north of the Croton Dam and other portions of the NCT didn't have their unequivocal magic when put into motion on a bike. They did and they will be missed.

Much can be said about the positions of the National Parks Service, USFS and various user groups, but the fact is the trail does not take or give anything to one group or another. It's simply there for those who choose to use it. That awakening of the spring, beauty of the fall colors or harsh unforgiving blanket of winter is there regardless of whether you're a hiker, skier or biker.

I hope you take the opportunity to discover the North Country Trail. Whatever method of travel you choose, please bring to the NCT a sense of wonder, an appreciation of its beauty and a respect for its wilderness-like solitude. For me it's this freedom of solitude that make each step I take or every circle of my wheel so special on the NCT.

I hope it's the same for you.

Dwain Abramowski
Executive Director
Michigan Mountain Bike Association

M-20 to Nichols Lake

County: Newaygo
Distance: 19 miles
Terrain: Wooded and rolling hills
Fees: none
Difficulty: Moderate

Segments of the North Country Trail are some of the most beautiful trails in Michigan, and for mountain bikers they're woodland riding at its best. The forest scenery is diverse and the number of people who venture onto the NCT, either bikers or hikers, relatively low. In short, the NCT is one of best places to experience that "freedom in solitude."

This segment describes a 19-mile ride from M-20 north to Nichols Lake. It is important to note that some Forest Service maps put the distance at 16.8 miles, but let me assure you it's a solid 19 miles.

Overall the ride is rated "moderate" with some short slopes and hills that beginners may have to hike up or down. Experienced riders will find the entire trail an easy ride with the exception of a few narrow bridges. Keep in mind that the NCT is popular with hikers and that all mountain bikers should be prepared to stop for pedestrian traffic. The NCT south of M-20 to the Croton Dam is closed to mountain biking.

There are no facilities at the trailhead on M-20 nor along the trail. Several campgrounds, including Minnie Pond in the Manistee National Forest, are located near the trail and can be easily reached by following secondary roads.

Getting There: From White Cloud head north on M-37 and then west M-20. You reach the trailhead within 2 miles.

Information: Contact Baldwin Ranger District, 650 N. Michigan, Drawer D, Baldwin, MI 49304; ☎ (616) 745-4631.

Heading north from M-20, there are a lot of small, well used two-tracks, logging and access roads that cross the trail from east to west. The first such road is reached within a third of a mile and another at **Mile 0.7**. Be careful crossing these roads as they are used on a regular basis.

At **Mile 1.2** the trail arrives at its first creek and you'll have to walk your bike across because the bridge is too narrow to ride. Just beyond the steep bank of the creek, the trail crosses another two-track and then a maintained dirt road before entering a stand of pines that provides some gentle up and down riding.

At **Mile 3.3**, you cross 3 Mile Road. By heading east on this paved road you'll reach Gordon Road, which can then be followed south back to M-20 and the trailhead for a 6.3-mile loop.

Continuing north on the NCT, you cross five two-tracks in the next two miles. The fifth one is at **Mile 6.5** and on the other side the trail climbs a steep ridge that skirts a series of bogs and small swampy lakes. After a couple of more two-tracks, the trail traverses wooded hills bordering some lakes and then arrives at a red gate. The gate marks a tract of private property and the NCT swings east of it.

Menna Creek is crossed via a wooden bridge and a half mile later you reach 6 Mile Road just past **Mile 9** of the ride. Head

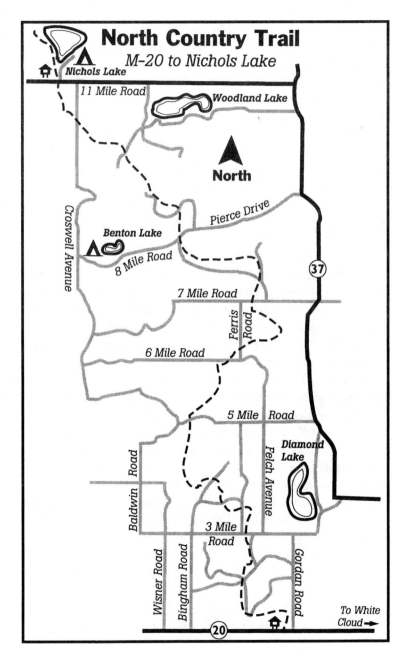

east on the gravel road for 200 feet to pick-up the trail and continue your ride north. Alternatively, you could take 6 Mile Road east to Felch Avenue and then head south to 3 Mile Road. Pick up Gordon Road to the east which will lead south to M-20. This will create an 18-mile loop of both winding, classic single track and scenic forested roads.

The NCT continues north as a high, dry ribbon around a swampy area and then crosses a series of two-tracks. The sixth one is reached at *Mile 12.4*. After that you enjoy the longest portion of trail without access roads or two-tracks, more than 2 miles of nothing but trees. For the first time that day you get a sense of being "in the woods" as the lightly used trail winds across a series of forested hills.

At *Mile 14.5,* be alert! The trail here follows a two-track road for several hundred feet along its west side and then turns sharply back into the woods. Within a half mile you emerge at an intersection with 8 Mile Road. At this point, the NCT follows an old access road, now closed to motorized vehicles, that heads north from 8 Mile Road. Also here, you'll hit the first major patch of sand in the ride.

At *Mile 15.3*, you cross Bear Creek. Again walk your bike here because the banks are extremely steep and the bridge is very narrow. The trail immediately crosses another gravel road and then at *Mile 16.6* reaches Michigan Creek. This is a scenic spot as the creek runs through a grove of large almost magical, cedar trees and is crossed by a long narrow bridge. Within a mile you cross Tank Creek and then Croswell Avenue at *Mile 17.8*.

Within a half mile, or at *Mile 18.2*, you reach 11 Mile Road where on the north side is Nichols Lake Campground and dayuse area. This national forest campground has drinking water, rustic campsites, a beach and parking. This makes it ideal for a vehicle-drop. Another option is to ride back via the roads. Avoid M-37 since there can be considerable traffic on it. The best road route to M-20 is Croswell Avenue south to 6 Mile Road and then east to Felch Road to 3 Mile Road, Gordon Road and finally M-20.

Bowman Lake

County: Lake
Distance: 8.4 miles
Terrain: Wooded rolling hills
Fees: None
Difficulty: Moderate

This section of the North Country Trail runs north from the trailhead of the Bowman Lakes Foot Travel Area to Timber Creek Campground on US-10, a ride of 8.4 miles. It includes crossing the Pere Marquette River as well as following two dirt roads and a half mile of South Branch Road, which is paved.

The trail is well posted with gray diamonds, easy to follow and scenic. Bikers are not allowed to continue along the NCT south of 56th Street nor can they ride the trails of the Bowman Lake Foot Trail Area, which circle that picturesque little lake.

Near the south end of this segment is Bowman Bridge Campground, overlooking the Pere Marquette River and very popular with canoeists during the summer. At the north end is Timber Creek Campground. Both USFS campgrounds are rus-

243

tic and have picnic areas with vault toilets and water.

If you don't feel like backtracking the route, a good alternative is to begin at Bowman Lake Foot Travel Area and follow the NCT until it reaches 40th Street. Head east on 40th Street, which turns into Mac Road when it swings south and eventually intersects 56th Street, only a quarter mile east of the trailhead. This loop would be a 6-mile ride.

Getting There: To reach the trailhead to Bowman Lake Travel Area from M-37 in Baldwin head west on Seventh Street and follow it as it curves and becomes 56th Street. Within six miles you cross the Pere Marquette River and pass the entrance to Bowman Bridge Campground. The trailhead to the lake is reached in another mile.

Information: Contact the Baldwin Ranger District at ☎ (616) 745-4631.

In the parking area of the Bowman Lake Foot Travel Area is a display for the North Country Trail, including a large map. Next to it is a spur, marked by both gray diamonds for the NCT and blue diamonds for the Bowman Lake Trail. The access spur heads east to quickly merge with the NCT, which heads north to immediately skirt the base of a steep ridge. At **Mile 0.5**, you come to a junction.

To the west (left) is Bowman Lake Trail, marked by blue diamonds and off limits to mountain bikers. But you can drop your bike and follow it on foot over the ridge to quickly descend to Bowman Lake, a glacial depression that filled in with water when the ice melted. Its shoreline of steep ridges gives you the feeling of Northwoods seclusion even though you're only a half mile from where you left the car.

The NCT continues north as a right-hand spur to climb a ridge for a nice overview of the lake and then descends away from it. Just past **Mile 1**, the trail bottoms out in a pleasant wooded bowl, then resumes climbing.

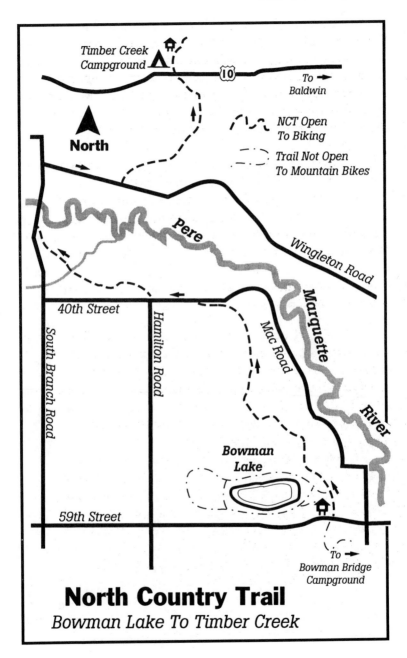

North Country Trail
Bowman Lake To Timber Creek

You gain more than 100 feet before the trail tops out. Within a half mile the NCT loses much of that elevation with a sharp descent and eventually swings west, parallels 40th Street briefly and then joins that dirt road at **Mile 3**.

The gray diamonds lead you west along 40th Street for a half mile until the intersection with Hamilton Road. At this point the NCT re-enters the woods but quickly emerges from the trees to cross a powerline right-of-way. On the other side it begins a gradual descent, reaching the edge of a high bank above a scenic stream at **Mile 4**.

You descend steeply to the stream, cross it on a wooden bridge and then climb the opposite bank. *Be prepared to get off your bike at the bottom as the bridge is too narrow to ride!* Once up the other side, the trail levels out, crosses an old two-track within a half mile and then arrives at a dirt road. The gray diamonds lead you around a gate and then along an overgrown two-track that descends towards the Pere Marquette River. Before reaching the river, the trail swings out onto South Branch Road.

Follow the paved road north as it crosses the Pere Marquette River. Located on the banks of the river here is an access site for canoers which includes vault toilets. The NCT continues along South Branch Road until **Mile 5.6** where it turns east onto Wingleton Road and follows the dirt road for almost a mile.

At **Mile 6.4**, the NCT departs Wingleton Road and begins as a level path through a pine plantation. Eventually you move into a hardwood forest along a trail that remains fairly level and easy to follow. Within a half mile of US-10, you skirt a low lying wet area in the forest and then begin a gradual climb. The trail crosses a gas line right-of-way, marked by bright yellow and red posts, resumes climbing and breaks out at the edge of a bank above US-10. *Be very careful crossing this road as it can be extremely busy with traffic!* On the other side the NCT resumes and at **Mile 8.4** reaches a spur to the Timber Creek Campground.

Timber Creek

County: Lake
Distance: 6.7 miles
Terrain: Wooded hills
Fees: None
Difficulty: Easy to moderate

This section of the North Country Trail begins at Timber Creek Campground along US-10 and heads north, reaching the Freesoil trailhead in 19 miles. Excellent views are enjoyed within 7 miles of the route, making the first section an ideal out-and-back ride of 13.4 miles. Despite the wooded hills, most beginners will be able to handle the ride if they keep in mind the fairly steep climbs encountered near Mile 6.

Facilities at Timber Creek Campground include trailhead parking area, vault toilets, water and rustic campsites.

Getting There: From Baldwin, head north on M-37 and then west on US-10. The campground will be reached within eight miles and is on the north side of the road.

Information: Contact the Baldwin Ranger District, 650 N. Michigan Ave. Drawer D, Baldwin, MI 49601; ☎ (616) 745-4631.

From Timber Creek Campground, there is an access spur that heads east and in a few hundred yards reaches the North Country Trail, where you can head north or south. To the south the NCT crosses US-10 (see Bowman Lake To Timber Creek ride).

Heading north, the NCT is a narrow path that sees a lot less use than most other segments. The trail gently rolls through hardwoods, pine plantations and along short sections of abandoned logging roads. There are few noticeable climbs for the first few miles even though the terrain overall is gently rising. After crossing several snowmobile and ORV trails, you reach 8th Street, a well established dirt road, at *Mile 3.7*. The trail is well marked on the other side of the road and continues north with an immediate climb.

From this point on, the North Country Trail enters much more challenging terrain, including a steady climb of more than 1.5 miles. This particular climb is less than a mile in length, but will still get your heart rate up. The view from the top is well worth the effort, especially in the early spring and late fall when there is little foliage. On a clear day you may see Lake Michigan, near Ludington, to the west.

For many mountain bikers the view makes this a good spot to turn around and head back for a total ride of a little more than 6 miles. You won't be disappointed, however, if you do travel on. In the late fall, you will be treated to additional views of wooded valleys and huge trees that rise from below like pillars holding up the sky.

Unless you like to kiss bark, you'll want to keep your speed well down in your comfort zone and just enjoy the view. At *Mile 6.7*, you'll come to FR-5196 (also called Centerline Road). The ride back to Timber Creek Campground from here will make a round trip of 13.4 miles.

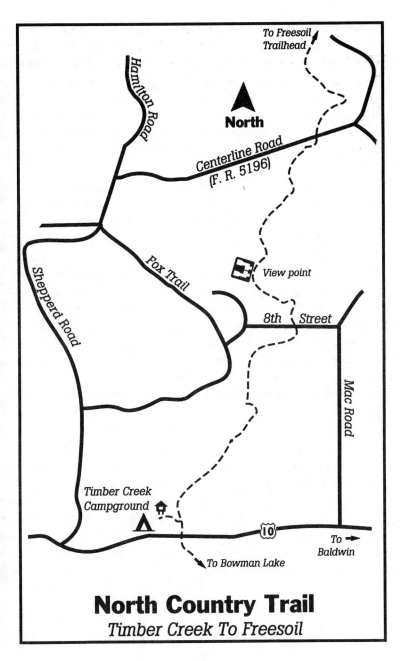

North Country Trail
Timber Creek To Freesoil

There are no mountains in southern Michigan but mountain bikers will find the off-road riding surprisingly rugged and technical at times.

Other Trails

Robinette's Apple Haus

The trails at Robinette's Apple Haus receive the heaviest use during races but people who only ride this Kent County mountain bike area on those days are missing a real treat. In the early spring, the trails wind past apple orchards in bloom and the sights and smells of the apple blossoms will fill your senses. The riding can be equally pleasant in the fall when red and green apples are crowding the branches.

Although the farm borders busy East Belt Line Avenue, there are still many places along the trails to lose sight of the nearby urban sprawl. The terrain features ponds, forested ravines and ridges, open fields and, of course, the perfect rows of the orchards. There is a total of 4.5 miles of trails at Robinette's, ranging from technical short climbs in the woods to all out speed runs on two-track roads through the orchards. For after the ride, there is a restaurant on site, with some of the best baked goods and hot cider to be found anywhere on the west side of the state.

Getting There: From I-96 in Grand Rapids, depart at exit 38 and head north on East Belt Line Avenue for 5 miles. At the corner of East Belt Line Avenue and Four Mile Road are signs marking the entrance of Robinette's.

Information: Contact Robinette's Apple Haus, 3142 Four Mile Rd., Grand Rapids, MI; ☎ (616) 361-5567.

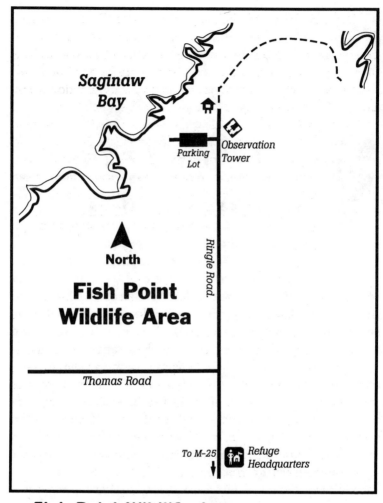

Saginaw
Bay

Parking
Lot

Observation
Tower

North

Ringle Road

**Fish Point
Wildlife Area**

Thomas Road

To M-25   Refuge
Headquarters

Fish Point Wildlife Area

Located on Saginaw Bay in Tuscola County, Fish Point Wildlife
Area is a 3,000-acre state game area that attracts thousands of
migrating waterfowl and swans in the spring and fall. A short but
enjoyable outing is to ride the 1.1-mile causeway along the Point,
stopping often to search the marshes and skies for a variety of
ducks and geese.

Don't be fooled by the short distance of this trail because Fish Point is a rewarding ride for non-aerobic reasons and can be combined use with Sleeper State Park's trails and a scenic tour on Sand Road in the Rush Lake State Game Area for a full workout. There are no fees or permits to use the trail or observation tower but Fish Point is only open from the end of April to Oct. I.

Getting There: From Bay City head east on M-25 east for 10 miles to Ringle Road. Head north on Tingle Road and the pavement will end in a little more than 2 miles at Gotham Road. Continue following the dirt road north to the observation tower and main parking area. The trail head is just north of the observation tower where there is a gate with trail information on it.

Information: Contact Fish Point Wildlife Area, 7750 Ringle Road, Unionville, MI 48767; ☎ (517) 674-2511.

Pando Ski Center

Located in Kent County near Rockford Pando Ski Center has developed 4 miles of single track and two-track trails in a terrain of wooded hills and open ski slopes.

In the past, the ski area has tried to get into the mountain biking mainstream in a variety of different ways, including hosting races since the mid-1980s, expanding its trail system and staging open riding periods one summer for a small trail fee. Except for the races, none of the other endeavors were successful. Currently the area is closed to mountain biking except on race days in the spring and summer but call for more information as trail activities could change in the future.

Getting There: From I-96 in Grand Rapids, depart at exit 38 and head north on M-44 (East Belt Line Avenue). After crossing the Grand River, M-44 swings east as Belding Road. Continue east on M-44 for 5 miles to reach the entrance of the ski on the south side of the road.

Information: Contact the Pando Ski Center, 8076 Belding Rd., Rockford, MI; ☎ (616) 874-8343. For the dates of races you can also contact Fun Promotions, P.O. Box 1383, Grand Rapids, MI 49501; ☎ (616) 453-4245.

Proud Lake Recreation Area

Proud Lake Recreation Area has plans to develop a mile-long mountain bike trail in conjunction with Association of Retarded Citizens and the Michigan Mountain Biking Association. Designed to accommodate beginners, the trail will be relatively flat and short path through beautiful wets lands. It will appeal to anyone seeking less challenging terrain, such as families and groups of mixed biking skills. Off-road wheelchair users and people with other physical challenges can also spend some quality nature time on this short trail.

Getting There: From I-96, east of Brighton, depart at exit 155 and head north on Wixom Road for 1.5 miles. Turn right on Pontiac Trail and then left immediately at the light to resume northbound on Wixom. After 2.5 miles turn right onto Glengary Road and follow it east 2 miles to Bernstein Road. Within a mile signs for the boat launch appear, directing you to turn left on Bass Lake Road. Where Bass Lake Road turns sharply north is the park access road to the boat launch. The trailhead will be on the edge of the woods on west side of the parking lot at the end.

Information: Contact Proud Lake Recreation Area, 3540 Wixom Road, Milford, MI 48382; ☎ (810) 685-2433

Brighton Recreation Area

Currently a new mountian bike trail is being constructed in the Brighton Recreation Area that will eventually replace the trail system presently being used. When that happens Penosha Trail and Kachin Trail will be open only to hikers.

The new mountain biking trail is expected to be 10 to 15 miles in length with a good portion built and ready to ride by the end of 1997. This new trail will run through the same forrested terrain as the hiking paths but will be better designed for mountain biking.

Call Brighton Recreation Area at ☎ (810) 229-6566 to see if the complete conversion has taken place.

The Authors

Sandra Davison

Sandra Davison grew up in Michigan and, with the exception of a short stint in Colarado, has been bicycling around the two peninsulas for the last few decades. Mountain biking since 1980, when equipment and trail access were scarce, she currently lives in central Michigan where some of the best trails in the state are only an hour from her home.

Her favorite character-building MTB experience was a 40-mile ride along the High Country Pathway where a compass was needed to get everyone out before total darkness set in. More recently she began racing tandem mountain bikes off-road because it's different, they go fast and most people wouldn't even try it!

Davison is the vice president of the Mid-State Chapter of the Michigan Mountain Biking Association and helped design the first phase of the Chief Cob-Moo-Sa Trail in the Ionia Recreation Area. She is a professional photographer and artist with illustrations in cookbooks, T-shirts and newsletters. She writes about biking, women in sports, nature and life.

Dwain Abramowski

Dwain Abramowski, is a published author as well as a free-lance writer, who has contributed articles and photographs to *Bicycling Magazine*, *Bike Magazine*, *Michigan Cyclist* as well as many other recreational magazines and newspapers. Abramowski was also one of the founders of the Michigan Mountain Biking Association in 1990 and served as the first MMBA president. He is currently the MMBA executive director and publishes the *Bent Rim Bugle*, the association's newsletter.

Abramowski is active in forest related activities in Michigan and serves on the Friends of the Forest Committee-U.S. Forest service for the Huron/Manistee National Forests, the State Forest Recreational Advisement Committee for the Michigan Department of Natural Resources State Forest Division, Chairs the Recreational Trails Advisement Committee for the the DNR and consults various regional and local units of government and private institutions on trail development and management.

Abramowski is also Michigan's International Mountain Biking Association (IMBA) representative as well as a Member of the Regional board for IMBA working with RIDE Inc., which assists to coordinate trail development and management activities in surrounding states.